Alice
the
Palace

Flaming Janet
Shadow of Palaces
Marjorie of Scotland
Here Lies Margot
Maddalena
Forget Not Ariadne
Julia
The Devil of Aske
The Malvie Inheritance
The Incumbent
Whitton's Folly
Norah Stroyan
The Green Salamander
Tsar's Woman
Homage to a Rose
Stranger's Forest
Daneclere
Daughter of Midnight
Fire Opal
Knock at a Star
A Place of Ravens
This Rough Beginning
The House of Cray
The Fairest One of All
Duchess Cain
Bride of Ae
The Copper-Haired
   Marshal
Still Blooms the Rose

The Governess
Children of Lucifer
Sable for the Count
My Lady Glamis
Venables
The Sisters
Digby
Fenfallow
The Sutburys
Jeannie Urquhart
The Woman in the Cloak
Artemia
Trevithick
The Loves of Ginevra
Vollands
A Dark Star Passing
The Brocken
The Sword and the Flame
Mercer
The Silver Runaways
Angell & Sons
Aunt Lucy
O Madcap Duchess
The Parson's Children
The Man from the North
Journey Beyond Innocence
The Charmed Descent
The Inadvisable Marriages
Curtmantle

Alice the Palace

*A Particularly Important
Bull Terrier*

PAMELA HILL

**THE VINEYARD PRESS
LONDON**

ISBN 1 86121 001 9

The Vineyard Press
89a Winchester Street
Pimlico
London SW1V 4NU

1   3   5   7   9   10   8   6   4   2

Photoset in North Wales by
Derek Doyle & Associates, Mold, Clwyd.
Printed and bound in Great Britain by
WBC Book Manufacturers Limited,
Bridgend, Mid-Glamorgan.

For
John Hale
with thanks for everything

Author's Note

This is not a story about doggy ways, but about a personality. Those who do not know bull terriers may not believe some of it. Those who do will understand it and may well be able to cap some of the episodes with others of their own. I do not, however, think they will be better ones.

My thanks are due to Mr and Mrs John Carr for the use of their very rare print *Caesar's Wife*; to the Paul Mellon Centre; to Ken and Mary Morrow for both photographs and encouragement; and, as always, to my customary publishers, Robert Hale Limited, for all possible help not only over this book, but with others over the years. Finally, The Dogs' Home, Battersea, who play a part in Alice's story, have been as helpful as ever with anything to do with a dog.

P.H.

One

I AM a bull terrier, as stated. We do as we like, so unless you are a strong-minded person with a certain amount of muscle and an understanding nature, don't buy one.

I must however state at this point, to avoid misunderstanding, that neither I, nor any of my family, are to be classed as pit bulls. Some of these, though not all, have been bred macho in order to fight. It is not their fault and has got them into the newspapers. I have never met one, and have never been involved in fighting in my life; it would be most undignified. Nor have I bitten anyone or, in fact, anything except two car tyres on separate occasions when they were engaged in running me over. You will agree that this was understandable behaviour in the circumstances.

For some time after I was born I looked like a pig. I had a pink nose and my ears, for the time being, flopped. This is the case with all bull terrier puppies as before they are born, it makes matters tidier inside their mother, as several of us are generally packed together. I knew at once that the situation would improve, as my mother Ariadne, who was very beautiful, had ears that stuck up like the sails of a yacht, though of course I hadn't seen a yacht then. Later I was to discover that ears are for pricking up if you feel happy or devilish, and laid back if you are frightened, which can happen even to us, mostly when we are young. My mother had a black nose, which meant that she was experienced and wise. Mine took several years to darken.

My sire, whom I never saw as far as I know, was called Achilles after a famous warrior. I believe he was white like me. There are whites and brindles, and some like one kind and some the other. I have a small brindle feather over my right eye, but that is all. Some of my brothers and sisters had a black patch all the way round one or the other, which is very becoming. However we must take what we get.

When I was a few weeks old I was taken away and put on hand feeding in a separate kennel with my handsome brother Albert, who always made me feel slightly plain. He was white with red brindle patches all over, most unusual and striking. I must explain here that all our litters born by then had names beginning with A, for registration at the Kennel Club. After a time they had to come off it, as all the A's were used up except for names like Avalanche, which granted would have been all right for some. However by then I had gone to Scotland, and by the time I saw them all again they had got to letter N. That episode will be mentioned in proper course.

It wasn't long before Albert was spoken for, by some Germans who came along and said he was *gemütlich*. Besides being extremely handsome he was a trifle forward by nature and kissed everybody who came along, managing it somehow through the chain link fence. I prefer to wait and be sure I approve of people before I kiss them, except in one instance later on when somebody needed a wash. Albert, spectacular in his dark red patches, made ready to go to Germany, I suppose, but was still present during the events I am about to relate.

We used to play with one another when we felt like it and the weather was all right. When it wasn't, we went back into our kennel, which was kept heated and very clean and comfortable. Two women looked after us and their names were Vi and Marge. Vi made out the pedigrees and arranged the breeding and kept the books and used to show some of us and win championships. There are several champions in my ancestry, so I expect I am a snob. I did not, however, stay long enough to be shown. As for Marge, she used to clean us and the kennel up and bring us food, milk and meat and wheat germ and biscuits and honey. I am still crazy about honey.

Every day the kennel and run were washed out and when this was going on I used to see my relations, cousins and uncles and aunts and my mother, much bigger than I then was, wagging their tails in their separate quarters. In my particular family tails wag frequently. Everybody was kept as free from infection as possible and as people from outside bring it in on their feet, they would only be introduced to us if they were probably going to buy one of us. That was why, when I saw a strange woman on the outside walk with Vi and Marge one day, I knew she had come for me. I drew back against the kennel wall and watched Albert make a fool of himself poking through the mesh and kissing away at the woman's hand. 'Isn't he gorgeous?' said the woman, and I knew she liked Albert best, but he as I say was booked for Germany. I did not let the matter upset me too much, but remained on cool terms until I saw what was what. Vi and Marge and the woman looked at me, sitting with my back against the kennel wall. 'She knows something's going to happen,' Vi said. Marge undid the gate and came in and carried me out and I was given to the woman. She held me against her and I began to like her quite well, and thought perhaps she would get used to me and forget Albert. 'I brought a mohair blanket to put round her,' I heard her say, 'but I left it on the train.'

It was February and very cold – I had been born on Boxing Day – and Vi went away and came back with a piece of pale pink flannel and the woman wrapped it round me, which helped. 'Mohair would have got up her nose,' said Marge. Both she and Vi made kissing noises and said goodbye to me, and I went out in the woman's arms and my pink flannel. We waited for a taxi to take us to the train. By this time I had finally approved of The Woman and licked Her face. When you belong to somebody you spell them with capitals. She was pleased and held me tight until the taxi came.

We drove in it for a while and then caught the train and then another train, and She put me on a seat beside Her in an empty carriage. We travelled for what seemed a very long time and now and again She patted me and spoke to me and said my manners were very good. I have no doubt She expected me to wet the seat during all these hours, but I did not; I think because of my breeding, which is, as Vi used to say, royal.

I must do some more explaining here about bull terriers. There are dogs and dogs, but we are special. Not everyone can get on with us, and the ones who can't should think of something else. We were put together – everyone knows about it – in the days when there was bull-baiting, and the ordinary bulldogs had difficulty in hanging on, to the bulls I mean, with their blunt noses, which stopped their breathing. So we were developed at last by mating bulldogs to several other kinds of terrier over a very long time until our line would breed true, and now we have Roman noses and a little smile. We also have the faculty of fighting any other dog for as long as anyone likes; our smiling jaws are very powerful, and in the old times, which were cruel, they used to crop our ears so that they wouldn't be caught at in a fight, and they would show customers how we could hang on to a bull's side and not drop off even when we were cut in half. They sometimes made us fight each other as well, for bets. I am glad I was not alive then; nowadays it is much pleasanter, but for some reason people who meet me with Her in the street often ask 'Is that a bulldog?' I look like one, I dare say, from the front except for my face. Other people sometimes call us English bull terriers. This is superfluous. Certainly there is a dotted line in the ancestry where they did something or other to produce a kind of cousin in Staffordshire, who are darker and different about the face, lacking our Roman noses. They are good guard dogs and in nature resemble us slightly, but there is no question of which is a proper bull terrier.

As for Her, I really do think that by the time we got into the train She had forgotten all about Albert and liked me instead. 'I was going to try to think of a name for you,' She said, 'but you've got one already from the kennels and it suits you. You are Alice. Alice the Palace. That makes poetry. What do you think?'

Ever since then She has got into the way of calling from a distance, not that I commonly go away far, Alice the Palace, which has a good echo to it. It sounds even better than Bill Bailey Won't You Please Come Home.

To return to the train journey. After a long time listening to the thump, drrr, thump of the engine and a lot of things going past outside, She said: 'Here we are in Scotland,' and a good while after that we got out at last and found Her car, which She had left at the station to meet us as it is a very long journey except by train. I got a walk then and was able to oblige, which was a relief. Presently I was put in the car and when it started to move, discovered that I liked it. I made it clear to Her at once that I must sit in front, no nonsense about dog barriers. Sometimes I curl up and go to sleep while She is driving and probably did so on that occasion, but oftener I like to sit up straight waiting to nod, like royalty, which after all I am, and a lot of people come and pay their respects.

We drove through forests and over mountain roads and past a great shimmering sheet of water She said was a loch, which being from England I wouldn't be able to pronounce. Then we drove through a town with shops and a derelict railway station, and She said they'd axed it, otherwise we could have come all the way by train, and they hadn't meant to axe that one but one somewhere else, but had got the plans mixed up and began tearing up the railway lines while everybody was still arguing. I didn't care as I liked the car best. Then we came to more empty road and in the end, very carefully, turned up one which had grass up the middle for quite a long way. She said it was an old pilgrimage road and the grass was for ponies to eat while they went on, but the butcher wouldn't call now because the grass broke his axle. 'It's nice and peaceful,' She said, and that suited me.

In the end we came to Her cottage, which had lots of garden and in front, an apple tree, and no other houses for a long way across fields. When I was a bit older and the apples set to fruit I used to walk along the drystone wall and pick myself apples off the tree and eat them, and once a car – there weren't so many cars then – went past while I was doing this and everybody inside laughed. I like fruit. I will eat apples and bananas and raisins and dates and figs, in fact whatever She eats. I could even fancy a drop of sherry, but She doesn't let me have it.

'I'm not going to show you, Alice, although you're quite good enough,' She said one day at the beginning, adding that it wasn't even a dog's life, it was a rat race. 'We'll have a nice quiet life up here instead, that's all,' She added. Some hopes, as I will describe in course of this narrative.

Meantime She told me stories of when She had shown other dogs, because of course I wasn't Her first as She is no chicken, although certainly Her first bull terrier. When She was a child She had always wanted a dog more than anything, but had never been allowed to have one, so as soon as it could be done She kept on buying them. One She used to show was a beautiful little black-and-white chihuahua named Magpie. These tiny dogs used to be kept in temples in Mexico, and when you die – She told me this – they light you across the nine dark rivers with their great shining eyes. I haven't got shining eyes as mine were bred to be small in my head, so I shan't be lighting anybody. However She went on to say that She hadn't realised that people who show small dogs have small minds to match. 'You wouldn't believe what went on,' She said, and told me a great many things I will not put down as otherwise certain sub-sections of the dog world

would sue us for libel. Firstly, persons showing chihuahuas – they are generally women – tend not to wear tough old clothes like everybody else in the rings, but dress themselves up as though it was a garden party in high heels and flowered hats with veils, and a hatpin to fasten the latter securely in case the chihuahua gets out of control. There was one notable exception whom She called The Bottom.

The Bottom was very fat with short legs. She always wore a shape-hugging jersey and royal blue transparent stretch tights with nothing on underneath, and took up a great deal more room than her chihuahua. Her bottom swung about independently with separate directions of its own, like a ship's boom or, as She muttered, a barrage balloon directed by radar. By then I didn't know what She was talking about, but at every single show they attended, She and Magpie seemed to land next door to this woman in the ring. Just as the judge came round The Bottom would swing with deadly accuracy to obscure any possible view of Magpie and, which is more difficult, of Her as well. 'I used to want to ask somebody for their hatpin to try and puncture it, but it would have exploded,' She said, adding that that was nothing to what some of them were doing on the sly, mostly beforehand.

Altogether, when Magpie died, She went into mourning for a bit and then decided to try to show the largest possible dog instead of the smallest, because perhaps they would have larger minds and smaller bottoms, so She got a mastiff. This is an ancient breed the Romans found when they came to Britain and were so impressed they took some back to Rome. They are extremely large, but in fact a Great Dane would have been taller, only She didn't find out in time and had meanwhile got very fond of the mastiff; he was fawn with a dark mask and was called Janus. 'He was like you, didn't take to what he wasn't used to at once, you had to get him to know you,' She said. In other words mastiffs, like bull terriers, do not hobnob.

Janus won a mention in his first puppy class and the judge said she'd fallen for him hook, line and sinker. After the class She overheard some woman in the next box, whose mastiff hadn't been mentined, making spiteful remarks about Janus' wishbone or some other part of him, and realised that the size of dog is nothing to do with it. It didn't matter, and She entered Janus, when he was a bit older and the size of a cottage piano, for the Daily Express Puppy Stakes at Olympia.

Now, London is not the easiest place in the world to find room for a very large dog, and at first they wouldn't let them into the hotel She had booked because She had only asked about a dog, not a pantechnicon. She promised to do better next time and they let them stay, but when She tried to get a taxi to Olympia next day – they had come down by train – the taxi driver was scared stiff and said 'Has he had his dinner?' In the end She got there safely, and met an uncle of hers who lived in town by himself, and didn't much like dogs anyway, so She left him with a large bottle of wine at the show bench while She and Janus went into the ring with dozens of other mastiffs from all over England. It was a great occasion, because the breed had almost died out and was reviving. Everybody hoped to win a rosette and, in that instance, a good deal of money, but only one dog could.

They began to go round and round before the judge, and this time even The Bottom could have done nothing at all about it. However a worse thing happened; at that point, She found to her horror that Her own tights were snaking down. It is not the kind of thing anyone wants to happen at the best of times, but with a mastiff on the end of a lead and photographers snapping away there was absolutely nothing to be done even by self-hypnosis. 'I didn't have a safety pin,' She said, 'and even if I had, it was a bit public.' Her uncle was far away with the bottle of wine and in any case would have been no help.

In the end, moving round and round in steadily increasing unease, She spotted a welcome sign not far off which said LADIES. She edged towards it out of the main stream, and immediately the steward came over and said, 'Do you want to stay in the class, madam?' She said She did, but was too backward to explain and anyway he wasn't the kind of man who would have a pin behind his lapel as some do in emergencies.

The situation became more acute, and She tried the same thing next time they got round there and the steward pounced again and said the same thing. So did She, as She is not easily defeated and had come all the way from Scotland to try to prove that Janus was the finest mastiff in the world. However at the third venture She simply dived towards the sign without waiting for the steward to say anything, and got inside somehow with Janus blocking the doorway and put in a fisherman's knot or whatever it is people put in when their tights are like concertinas. They came back safely, but by this time Janus was getting bored, for which nobody can blame him. The class went on for three hours, and by the time the judge came at last to look at Janus in particular he simply sat down as much as to say that was that. They didn't win a rosette or

even a mention, let alone the fare, and when She got back to the bench her uncle had drunk all the wine.

It turned out to be very sad about Janus as he died at only three years old. 'He would never body up,' She said. 'He had nephritis and I couldn't feed him red meat. He caught it when he was young, or else inherited it. There were only nine mastiffs left in Britain after the war and they're all inbred by now. They are trying to make them stronger by interbreeding with bull mastiffs.'

I looked superior, because exactly the same kind of thing has been done with bull terriers, as I have explained.

It was after that She came south and found me. Somebody had told her she wouldn't be able to cope with a bull terrier. That was enough to set Her off. It turned out, for once, that She had been right and the other person wrong. This is a great comfort to consider.

Two

There isn't much to say about those first days because
we were happy, and when you are happy you don't
notice time go by. My ears began to cheer up, but
before that a man in a wheelchair bowled up to the
door with an Alsatian running beside him. He was
called the Major, although She called him Michael.
He had the bluest eyes ever seen, like gimlets, and
red hair turning grey, and he smoked cigarettes one
after the other in an ivory holder and then threw
away the stubs. She told me afterwards Janus used to
eat the stubs, but I wasn't going to. I wondered why
the Major didn't get out of his electric chair and walk
about or come in. It turned out that he couldn't, as he
had been an invalid since the war. He had been a
brilliant officer, the youngest major in the Army at
twenty-two, in fact such a good artillery instructor
they wouldn't release him to go and fight. He went
on pestering them until they did, and at last they sent

him to the Middle East, and as soon as he got there he caught polio, was sent straight back to England to hospital and never walked again. He did all sorts of other things instead; played top flight bridge, owned racehorses, placed bets, drove a Bentley with hand controls but wouldn't bring it up our road, and otherwise got about in the chair, which ran on electric batteries which were always going flat. When he was stuck in the middle of nowhere as a result, he used to fire a pistol and his man, who had been a batman, would come and tow him away in a tractor, because the Major also had a farm, about two miles from Her cottage.

I took all this as it came, but what I was not at all sure about was the Alsatian. She was a bitch, and bitches are never nice to one another, just like women. On that first visit She kept me up in Her arms because I hadn't had my injections, being still too young, but later on, as soon as that bitch could get at me, she bit me twice on the shoulder. I had just been getting over the first bite when the second happened, and the hair never grew back again, so it was as well She hadn't meant to show me. All the Major did about it was laugh. He laughed as well when he saw me that first time, and She spoke up.

'You told me I would never control a bull terrier, so here she is,' She said. He looked superior and said she had been very wise to get a bitch as she would never have controlled a dog. Then he looked me over and suddenly spoke very gently.

'I never thought I'd see one again,' he said. 'Hello, Alice.'

I learned later that he had always had bull terriers in the days when he could walk. One was called Tony and was so temperamental nobody else could deal with him. 'I took him along with me in the regiment, and there was another there, and we used to get them to fight and put bets on. It was good fun.'

'Well, there isn't going to be any fun of that kind here,' She said firmly, and took me out of the way for the time being. After the Major had gone She told me the Alsatian had torn out a tuft of Her hair when she was waiting for him once in his sitting room to watch television, which as a rule She hates, and had reached over meantime to take a magazine from a side table. There is no doubt Alsatians are good guards, but so am I.

One way and another that one never did take to me. It may partly have been a matter of colour. She liked Biddy best, and Biddy was black as black. I have not got to her yet but she is coming along.

She told me afterwards that the Alsatian was a guard in case anyone tried to rob the Major on the road in his electric chair, as he was paralysed from the shoulders down except for his fingers. A bull terrier – he had had Tony put down when he went to the Middle East – wouldn't have done anyway as they don't always go the way their owners want them to. Once Tony in his time had been waiting with the Major for a train at the beginning of the war before they did their axing, and decided that he would rather walk down the railway line in the opposite direction instead. The Major had had to chase after him for quite a long way while everybody stared and the train waited, and came back at last with Tony by the scruff of the neck and feeling, as he said, an absolute fool. By now, as he couldn't take anything by the scruff, the Alsatian was a better idea. They have two speeds, a loping one and a walking one. This one would sit in the back of the Bentley as well.

I said we were happy. The cottage stood on a narrow road bounded by fields, and in the fields were very special cattle owned and bred by the farmer on the low road, made long after ours. Some were shaggy Galloways, black or dun, and others were Herefords with light eyelashes, and some were a mixture of the two and didn't look like anything in particular. There was an enormous Hereford bull. I have mentioned already that my ancestors were bred to bait bulls, and I once ran after this one. I wasn't interested in the cows. I chased the great wobbling bull until he suddenly took thought to himself and turned round and looked at me, so I thought I'd better beat it. When I got back She said to me that it was a good thing I hadn't done him any harm as he was worth several

thousand pounds. 'And for any sake,' She said, 'don't chase the sheep.' There were a few of those, silly woolly things, but again I wasn't interested. The farmer was a nice farmer, which they aren't all by any means, and didn't mind if I mooched about in his fields. There were good boggy bits Biddy liked later on, though I myself don't like getting my feet wet, and then and later mostly stayed on the little hillocks with gorse on, where rabbits and hares were. Rabbits are as stupid as sheep but I must admit I have never managed to catch one. Speed is a capacity I only reach for cats, as will be related. As for the hares, they run in a circle so all you have to do is wait, if you have any common sense, then they come haring back. However I did not molest them, being very well fed already. It was nice at the cottage, with the garden and the fields and the apple tree and peace. I still think of it sometimes, as it didn't last.

We used to go together, She and I, either down the

27

road or up, as there were no side turnings, except for one to the upper hill farm. The pilgrims used to come all the way from Edinburgh on foot long ago, and some of them were kings. They crossed a ford near the Major's farm, which is bounded by old willows down where the river runs, and came on up to where we are, where She got her water supply at first from a saint's well which never ran dry. Later She was put on the mains which had much nastier water, but at the time I speak of that had not yet happened, and is called progress. Our own road, when we went up it, ended in a pig pen because the nice farmer had locked off the right-of-way, which he shouldn't have, but nobody bothered to stop him in five years so by that time it was legal. Otherwise we could have walked all the way across to Wigtown. The pilgrims had gone even further, to St. Ninian's shrine in Whithorn, which made a very long walk.

There were no pigs in the pig pen anyway because bacon prices were low, which brings me to something that happened quite early on, before my ears started absolutely and permanently to rise.

One day when we were walking a car stopped and a woman got out. I could tell from her smell that she wasn't a nice woman. There was a yellow dog sitting in the car and I knew at once that it didn't have any sort of a life. Its eyes were sad and when I barked, which in honour bound I must do on such occasions, there was no answer. The woman had her hair hidden in a sort of greasy headband. I didn't like her. Her eyes were like black-currant jelly and she was sleazy and white and blurred, like somebody seen under water.

'I say,' she called to Her, 'I've just been to town and forgot to buy myself any brandy. Will you be going in and if so will you get me some?' She had to shout through my barking as I decidedly did not fancy her, and she started to shout at me, to which I am not accustomed.

'Doglet,' she said, 'stop making a noise. Quiet, doglet. Down, doglet' (I hadn't risen). 'Shut up, doglet, doglet, doglet,' I was insulted, naturally, and made more noise than ever and started skipping about and getting in her way. I may have resembled a pig at that stage as regarded my ears and pink nose, but I am by no means a piglet. They may have amiable natures but that is the only resemblance, as they have curly tails and noses made for rooting.

In the end She headed me off and told me in a mutter to pipe down and picked me up, because I was still small enough in those days, and said with Her nose in the air that She wasn't going into town, She'd been already. Afterwards She said to me: 'I'm glad you barked, Alice. She's a nasty bit of work and the grocer won't sell her any more brandy because she still hasn't paid for the last lot or the one before. She's usually drunk and she shouldn't be driving.'

All this might have been like water under the

bridge, but one night I was doing my mooch round the fields and had just got back – I never go far – and suddenly saw the lights of a car rocking slightly, and went to find out more. The next thing I knew was a violent crushing pain and the sound of brakes screeching. I rolled to the side of the road and the car went on, and I fled away from the road and the house and tried to lose myself in one of the fields. When the tyre had hit me I had yapped and snapped, not noises I generally make at all, and She came out of the house in a hurry and called: 'Alice, Alice.' I heard her but couldn't move. I was walking on three legs and something had happened to one of them. The pain had grown pretty bad and it was the first I had ever felt. I don't count the injections at the vet's, which were nothing worth mentioning.

She must have gone and got a torch which shone and picked out my eyes where I was hiding. She came and found me; I was hanging my head in a kind of shame, because I didn't understand what had happened and felt I shouldn't have let it. She carried me back over the stone wall and into the cottage, and telephoned the vet. He came out and I smelled the smell of operations about him and didn't like it, but he was very careful in the way he handled me.

At last he said 'The front left leg's broken, crushed at the shoulder. Didn't the driver stop?'

'Not her. Can you set it tonight if I come down to

the surgery with Alice?' However he said it was a complicated fracture and it wouldn't do any harm to leave it for a few hours, and he would make arrangements with a very special veterinary college near Glasgow where they had things his surgery hadn't. So next day I set out with Her in Her car, wrapped in the mohair rug She'd managed to get back from the railway people, and it didn't get up my nose and I would hardly have noticed if it had, having other things to worry about.

We drove and drove, and at last came to a fearful thing called a cattle grid. I do not know why, but though I will face most things I will *not* drive over a grid; the metal bars make sounds like something growling. Later on She used to let me out of the car when we came to one, drive over it and come back for me and tell me not to be a fool. Meantime, I dived on my three remaining legs down between the brake and the clutch to get at Her feet and feel safe. It almost caused an accident, of course. She had to stop with the handbrake and was cross with me for moments and I was miserable accordingly, but She isn't cross for long and told me it was the entrance to the college and soon I would be quite all right again.

Soon a girl in a white coat gave me an injection which put me right out and next thing I knew I was lying on my side in a cage and my shoulder ached and stung and had twelve stitches in it, not to mention what must have been done inside. They had to put in

31

a metal spiral and a metal pin, and it worked all right sooner or later although I have never since been quite as symmetrical as I had started out. They liked me very much at the college and would have made friends with me if I had felt inclined, but I didn't and mostly pretended to be asleep. They told me She kept ringing up on the telephone to ask how I was getting on and when She could have me back.

Soon She called back for me and took me away, and I was glad. Our own vet was to take the stitches out in about ten days, and a week after that I was to be brought back for checking up with another X-ray, which meant the cattle grid again. I mention all this not because the bones didn't heal, they did in a way: but it did something to my mind. I had learned that you don't rush at cars, which is useful although not many came up our particular road, it was too grassy then. I may mention at this point that shortly after all that the drunk woman was caught driving under the influence and was banned for six years, which meant she couldn't come and bother us again over brandy or much else.

She hadn't really been cross, She said, about the matter of the grid, it was just that I had got on to the brake and She couldn't stop the car. Every time we met another cattle grid I went on in the same way and in the end She designed a seat belt for me made out of two leads and thick string. I was able to look quite dignified in it, sitting up in front, and I could still lie down when I wanted to and anyway we weren't arrested, like the drunk woman who had run me over.

Three

I dare say I had been a nuisance with the grid that time, but sometimes I am helpful because I notice things She doesn't. Once it was very cold and everything froze and I wasn't able to go out except on necessary business, and soon came in again. Then the thaw came and She sat at Her typewriter doing a spot of work to pay for my dog meat, which costs a bit. The typewriter went tap, tap and presently I began to hear another sound that went drip, drip, and I began to bark. She looked round, very cross. 'Haven't you learned to shut up while I'm typing?' She said. 'There isn't anyone at the door.' She got up and went to look, just to make sure, and came back and said I was a nuisance. 'There isn't any point in hitting you, it's like hitting concrete,' She said, which is true. The dripping noise still came and I went on barking, and in the end She stopped the typewriter and flung Her hands up in the air and said: 'What *is* the matter? I'll go and look,' and opened the kitchen door and there was a lot of water pouring down from the ceiling. She said the pipes had burst, or something, and went to the place where the water is turned off and presently the rain stopped, but not before it had wetted my favourite velvet armchair. She thanked me for my help and telephoned the plumber. He kept us waiting a long time and when he came at last said he was very sorry, but everyone else's pipes had burst at the same time. In fact he found a two-inch block of ice on top of the water tank where he'd forgotten to put the lid on, which might have been part of the reason. I like to think that the damage would have been much worse if I hadn't warned Her in time, and after that She always took me seriously when I barked about one thing and another, because I only bark when it is necessary, not like some dogs who yap all day for nothing.

All of that happened after the trouble about my sleeping arrangements had subsided. It wasn't real trouble, just give and take, which everybody has to observe in the ordinary way. The point is that when I am put on Her bed anywhere I have to sleep in the middle. It is a matter of honour, but it blocks Her circulation. 'If you were like other dogs you'd sit at the back of the car and sleep at the end of the bed, but you won't.' She said. As She is an insomniac we had to think of something else. At one point She bought a

dog sofa, but I wasn't interested; then She bought a bean bag, and that was great fun, though possibly not for Her. It was an enormous fat red sausage stuffed with something or other that moved with your shape when you sat down. It had a zip fastener, and the minute I was left alone with it I pulled at the handle of the zip and hundreds and hundreds of white foamy things fell out and bounced all over the room. I shouldn't have been surprised if She had been rather cross, but She only laughed and said; 'I suppose it's my fault for getting you in the first place,' and collected every single bean, as they are called, and put them back in and sewed everything up firmly so that even I could not do any damage. After that I sat on the bean bag till it got dirty, and as She could not bear the thought of emptying out all the beans again to wash the cover we left it for the dustman. They make them now with separate washable covers, but She didn't bother about it. By now I have my separate armchair, the brown velvet one, with my own blanket in my own room. There were complications even about this last. At first it was a nylon blanket that brought me out in spots, and after some very expensive treatment which included pills and a daily shampoo, She thought of giving me a woollen one. The spots went away and we all went to sleep in peace, at least up till the time of writing.

Of course in process of all the happenings related above, my ears had risen. They are magnificent now, as good as my mother's. It is possible to express all shades of feeling with ears, but I have said that already. Wherever we lived there was always a mirror against the wall where She could look at the hems of Her skirts to see that they were all right, and once I looked in it and saw a white dog with a brindled feather over one eye, but never again. I do not like mirrors; they show everything the wrong way round, and by now I refuse to look in them. In spite of the creeps that one look gave me I did see that my nose was beginning to turn black and also, by now, my mouth. It takes a very long time for a white bull terrier to get all the black bits it ought to get. My feet are small and delicate and look as if I wore high-heeled shoes. They help me never to knock anything over unless I mean to, in which case I do.

As regards knocking things over, She once came back with a stuffed lion cub called Balthasar from the

Army and Navy Stores in London to put on Her bed. I don't think She meant him as a companion for me and I must say he is singularly silent. He was kept in great awe and majesty until one day when I was watching and a mouse came into the room at the cottage and jumped up to Balthasar and nibbled some stitches out of his face, which began to fall to pieces, and took away some of the stuffing inside to make a nest. I laughed and laughed to myself but when She came back She was in great distrees. 'You were so beautiful,' She complained, and took a needle and thread and some cotton wool and mended his face, but it is still a bit lopsided, like I am. I don't mind Balthasar's company when I am alone, and I play a game with him which means knocking him about a bit, like one of Cromwell's ruins in the song. A bullseye is when I get him turned upside down with his tail in the air and his head in one of Her slippers.

It is only very seldom that She has to part with me as a rule. When She goes abroad to places like France and Vienna I can't go, or rather couldn't come back if I did without spending six months in quarantine because of Customs regulations about rabies. The first time She went was just after I got my spiral tin shoulder and She took me back to stay with Vi and Marge for a few days. They told me I'd been very brave, but that after all is what is expected of a bull terrier. It was interesting to see some of my relations again, but I didn't get near them as they are still kept as free from outside infection as possible. My mother had had other litters meantime and didn't know me from Eve.

I was kept in the house as an honoured guest, and given a nice tea chest to live in with more pink flannel at the bottom to keep me warm. There was a tiny chihuahua there all the time by then. I will say he was as brave as I am, in spite of being so much smaller than any other dog. They aren't silly at all, but boast distinguished ancestry and have the great advantage that they can jump on sofas and things of that kind without anyone's minding. That particular chihuahua tried to impress me with the tale that as temple dogs they still had the privilege of ferrying their owners' souls across the nine dark rivers, but I said I'd heard it already.

When She came back I was very pleased to see Her and we drove straight home. She said She was glad to be there as the food in France had been very bad as they didn't like British tourists, and She said She would never go there again and everything was so expensive She had only been able to bring home one tiny heart-shaped pottery ashtray in the blue and brown Norman pattern with wriggles and flowers, and as She doesn't smoke I don't know why She even brought that.

Next time she went to Austria, and came back in a yellow hat with feathers on. I had by then been in a very nice kennels outside London with indoor heating and two friendly Alsatians and a pony and a donkey and a ghost, but I was glad to see Her again.

Four

I want to describe that kennels, because it was run by very, very nice people. When Biddy was alive we used to go to one in Scotland together while She went away; it was all right, but nothing special, and not for too long. After we were in London, however, She began to get delusions of grandeur and discovered cousins in Canada and went to visit them, and once went another time on a cruise. This was all very well for Her, but not fair to Me. However the new kennels people were wonderful and liked me especially although they had plenty of other dogs to look after, as they have a very good reputation. She didn't have a car by then, and they used to come and collect me in their estate car with my usual blanket under me to let me know I hadn't gone for good. It was quite different from travelling in a police van with picked-up strays, which has also happened and I am unlikely to forget it.

The grub was good in the kennels and as I always do, I kept myself to myself. There weren't any other bull terriers and Sheila, the owner's wife, used to come and talk to me. The days went on, and at night an odd thing used sometimes to happen. They were using a pile of old bricks to rebuild a summer-house in the garden, and the bricks were so special they'd brought them with them from their last house. A woman would appear sitting on them, and although it was dark I could see her clearly. She wasn't dressed like anyone nowadays, not even Her when She dresses herself up to go out somewhere in the evening. This woman wore a flat white headdress and a long gown of dark red, and I knew her name was Mary Sykes. She hadn't said so, and didn't bother me, and none of the other dogs made any noise as they would have done when anyone visited the kennels from outside. She simply sat there, and sometimes she went away.

One day Sheila came to groom me, and I saw scratches on her arms. The kennelmaid was there as well, sweeping out, and I heard Sheila say 'Mary Sykes came in last night and scratched me in bed again. She never touches Mark.' Mark was Sheila's husband.

The kennelmaid didn't seem surprised, and Sheila went on to say that Mary Sykes said she'd died in childbirth in the reign of Mary Tudor. She had evidently followed them from the last house along with the Tudor bricks. I wagged my tail to show I understood, and Sheila said 'Yes, Alice, but we don't want it known because a ghost would be bad for business. We hoped we'd left her behind when we moved.' I have said nothing about it till now, but there it is.

Later on, when She returned from Her cruise, I was taken back to London, but didn't do my round-and-round dance of joy as I usually do, because I was cross with Her for staying so long away. I stood in front of Sheila instead and paid more attention to her than to Her. It worked, and when Sheila had gone She came and made a great fuss of me and said She was sorry She'd been so long away and it wouldn't happen again if She could help it. In fact, the next time was when She had to go into hospital, and She certainly couldn't help that, but it was later on.

I have described the cottage road, where cars seldom came up after the drunken woman had been gathered to her fathers. For a long time it stayed pleasantly stony with green up the middle for ponies and horses who never now came. Looking over the fields we could see – at least, I couldn't, as my eyes are near-sighted, but She used to talk about it – the Carse of Solway, with the river broadening out towards the sea, and mountains on the far side; it was absolutely peaceful. However at the top was a hill farm where after the drunken woman left, two nice women came who kept goats. They used to walk them down in the evenings because goats like different kinds of green stuff, not always the same thing. The goats were friendly and had little white fur bells on their necks. Sometimes people would come up to buy goat's milk, and one day we were walking along the road and a car drove slowly past and then stopped.

'Why, there's a bull terrier,' somebody said, and I was pleased because by now I knew that we are seldom seen in Scotland and it is pleasant when someone appreciates us. I looked round and saw that the car was full of other bull terriers and they were all looking at me. A man and woman got out and introduced themselves as Ken and Mary. They breed my kind of dog in North Humberside and also have a special place to take care of bull terriers who have been abandoned by their owners, sometimes driven miles from home and then dumped, not knowing where they are or where to go. Ken and Mary would take them in and look after them and, if they could, find them careful new homes. It seems to me (and to Her and them) such a dreadful, heartless thing to buy a puppy, enjoy it while it is playful, then when you are tired of it put it right out of your life. Bull terriers especially give their trust to one person and find it difficult to do the same again, so it is quite a job to rehabilitate them, as it is called. Sometimes Ken and Mary have as many as nine waifs at once and they are mostly dogs, not bitches, as dogs are very strong-willed and independent and a stupid or careless owner can't cope.

Something like that had happened to one of the dogs in the car. His name was Toughy and he was a very handsome brindle. He hadn't been found abandoned, but in his case it was probably worse. Bull terriers hate water, and Toughy's late owner had forced the dog to come skin-diving. By the time Ken and Mary got him he was almost crazy and very, very difficult. Ken saw that he was a very good dog indeed and by degrees, won his trust. After that he took all kinds of trouble with Toughy, took him everywhere, treated and fed him kindly, and by degrees – this is quite something – got him ready to show. That was why they had come; there was a local show at Wigtown, and Ken thought it wouldn't be too much of an ordeal by then for Toughy, to try him out. (I wasn't being shown, as apart from my squint shoulder and bald patch She is too lazy to be bothered after the matter of the concertinaed tights at Olympia). Anyhow, Toughy and a white bitch were brought out of the car on to our stony rutty road, and we all said how do you do, except that Ken held Toughy by the shoulders in case he got difficult, but he didn't. Later I heard that Toughy had won a prize at Wigtown. When we last heard he was almost a champion at Crufts and had won a great many rosettes and prizes. As I say, he was very handsome and I think they they might have liked me to marry him, but She had promised to arrange this with Vi and Marge when it came along. So we all said goodbye for the time, but they came up every year after that with Toughy, to see me and to enter him at the local show, which by then had grown big and important.

I expect Biddy was around somewhere then. I feel guilty when I think of her, so will do the explaining later on.

As regards my marriage. The first time I went in season I was not mated as I was too young. Nobody quite understood, accordingly, when I began to swell up and make milk. I was taken to the vet to see if I had made a *mésalliance*, which I knew I hadn't but nobody would believe me. The vet felt me all over and said: 'Ay, ay. Have you been a naughty girl?' which is not the kind of thing I am accustomed to

have said to me. We waited for six weeks or so and
nothing more happened, which I could have told
them if they had really wanted to know. Next time I
went in season was six months later, and She said
that if I was going to go on like it anyway we might as
well get me properly married. So we drove all the
way down to see Vi and Marge, and I did a thing I
only do on very, very special occasions; when Marge
came to the door I lay down flat on my stomach and
wagged my tail fit to bust. She was pleased to see me
too, but the regulations for getting married there are
very odd. First of all I was taken into a small room full
of boxes and shelves and a table, and put on the table,
and an object was fitted over my face. It was a muzzle
made of leather and they call it the bridal veil. Marge
then sat on my head as though I had been a horse. As
for Vi, she brought in the mate, a brindle, I
understand, at the other end. They called him
Nicholas and I never yet saw him. At first they
thought nothing was going to happen because
Nicholas was more interested in the next day's
dinner which was on one of the top shelves. I could
feel Her getting worried because we had driven all
that way down and it might be for nothing. She told
me afterwards that She then said a prayer to a very
important married saint and then it happened
without any trouble and Nicholas and I plighted our
troth according to schedule. Vi and Marge carried me
out immediately in a reclining position and laid me in

the car. Of course I sat up at once; don't know what else they expected. They seemed to think that I had lost what Nicholas had put in, but I hadn't. The whole business had been, in my view, a fuss about nothing. Anyway it worked.

When we got back home She told the wedding story to the Major and he laughed and laughed. He told the story to everyone in the place. 'You've dined out on it for about eighteen months,' She said to him one day. Whenever we met anyone at all after that they would eye me and say: 'Is this the dog with the marital troubles?' which was not a fair question as I hadn't given any trouble at all, and I would have liked at least to set eyes on my bridegroom.

I started to swell up and have milk again, but this time for the proper reason. The puppies were born in due course and there were eight of them, which is good going. They started to be born when I was upstairs and I rushed down and began to have them on a very expensive Chinese rug I had always liked. She came and said: 'Not there, if you don't mind,' and took me to her own bed where there were lots of lovely warm clean woollen blankets of a Parma violet colour trimmed with satin She'd saved up for with stamps. It was almost as good as the rug. By the time I'd finished it was evening and there was a mark right through all the blankets which would never come out. I got very busy licking the puppies clean and She helped me burst the bags over their noses. I was quite pleased with myself. None of them had a feather over one eye like me. One was a brindle like its unknown sire, and the others were white, some with a black eye, and one dog was white all over. The rest were bitches and when Vi heard she was disappointed. 'Everybody wants dogs,' she said over the telephone. As for Her, she was delighted with everything I'd done and almost decided to keep the little brindle bitch with us, but I said no. We took the litter out to show to the Major and that was that.

It seems a long time since I had the puppies. I fed them easily because I was bulging with milk, and they used to play about the floor and make nuisances of themselves, in fact the room didn't seem big enough and I began to get bored with them. I wasn't too sorry when the time came to take them back to Vi and Marge, who had promised to buy them. We went down the M6 and the M1 and if you want to imagine what it was like to drive all that way on a motorway in summer with nine bull terriers all barking their heads off, try it.

In fact it was sad after all to part with the puppies and see their faces looking out at me from the indoor run where they'd been put. I thought they were handsomer than the litter next door, who were a little older; but Vi said their heads weren't good and she had expected better things of me, and they all needed worming. However we knew she would be very particular as to who bought them, so we went away, and had a quiet journey north and I got my figure back in a few days the same as ever.

Once when we were driving along the back road down near the river a woman stood in the middle of the road waving her shopping bag. We thought there was something wrong but it turned out that she expected a lift, just like that, to Wigtown. I wasn't going to leave my place in front and she didn't get in at the back, so I sat on top of the handbrake between her and Her. It isn't often that She gives lifts as it can be dangerous and anyway She can't be bothered stopping and starting. However here we were with this customer and she smelt dreadfully. It wasn't the personal smell which some people have and can't help, although there are plenty of things at the chemist's for them to use if only they will. This was a smell of sheer dirt, years and years of it, and the air in the car began literally to hum. I could think of only one thing to do and I started to wash the woman's face the way I had used to do with the puppies, very thoroughly. She began to complain and said she didn't like dogs licking her face. All She said was: 'I'm driving, I'm afraid,' and drove grimly on – luckily it wasn't far – and we deposited the smelly woman at the butcher's. Since then She has never given a lift to anybody unless She knows them already. Afterwards we went home and She washed out my mouth and tongue with Dettolin and gave me a good sponge down and even cleaned the insides of my ears with cotton wool dipped in cleansing milk, so that they looked like rose petals.

That was after the Standard poodle, Biddy, had come and gone.

I should have mentioned Biddy before the part about my marriage and family, and most of the rest. The fact is I wanted to put her at the back of my mind and keep her there.

Why there had to be a second dog I do not know. Biddy was, as I have said, a Standard poodle. When she arrived she was small enough to fit into an embroidery basket and at first I thought she was a ball of black silky wool. Then when she saw me she screamed and a little pointed shaved face poked out of the bundle, and she screamed again when we were left by Her to spend the night together, saying we might as well start as we meant to go on. So there we were, Biddy and I, left alone with nothing to say in particular because there simply was nothing to be said. I was secretly very much offended. I had been the Only Dog and now here was an intruder, and I don't believe humans understand how much one's feelings can be hurt by such a happening. I wasn't very old by then and it was not that there was anything nasty about Biddy. In fact she was probably nicer than I was. She was affectionate and well mannered and no doubt beautiful, if you like a dog with a coat that tangles if it isn't brushed every day. Biddy had to have her face shaved, as I've said, and her paws and the root of her tail. By then you knew which end of her was which. By degrees we got used to each other's company, though nothing was quite the same. We used to be taken for walks together up the road and down. Biddy was much more energetic than I am and used to jump the stone walls round the fields. She never did chase sheep because she had been told not to, and as for the bull, she wasn't interested. She aimed to please. Once in the fields she would run round and round and round, enough to make even a hare dizzy. I didn't try to compete. The fields at the back stretched away up towards moor and more moor and there were no cows or sheep, only bracken and a few sloe bushes with white blossom in summer. It wasn't very exciting and I began to leave halfway on walks and go back and sit outside the cottage till She and Biddy got back.

One day the Major came in his chair. 'Where's this bloomin' poodle?' he asked; he hadn't thought it was a good idea to have two. However when Biddy appeared a strange thing happened; the Alsatian took a fancy to her. She had grown quite a bit by then and was almost bigger than the Alsatian and much bigger than I was, and the pair used to stand aside and chat and nose one another and play together quietly. I think it may have been because dark dogs like other dark dogs best. At any rate it left me in peace without having my shoulder mauled where the scar was.

Biddy grew and grew till she was the size of a Galloway calf. She could do some things I couldn't; she could climb, she could jump on a table to be brushed, and she could waltz with Her when the wireless was turned on. Biddy and She used to waltz together round and round the room with Biddy's pink tongue lolling out because she was happy. A poodle is an affectionate creature and once Biddy had got used to the sight of me and I had made it clear that if she behaved herself there would be no trouble, we stayed civil, if cool.

I had to put up with a certain amount, however. Sometimes we used to drive down in the car, all three of us, to the Bishop's Burn, which in Scotland is the name for a stream. The burn was broad and sluggish and full of waterweed. We used to go down with Her into the field beside it and the Major would come along in his electric chair with his Alsatian, whose name was Heidi. All three of us dogs used to lollop – I can't think of a better word – through the long grass of the field towards the water. When it got to the water itself I stopped, naturally. I don't like getting wet at any time and certainly not on purpose. Biddy and Heidi, however, swam in the stream like a couple of otters, and then Biddy used to come back and shake her wet coat all over everything and soak it and me as well, and then go in again. It didn't look as if She minded, but sometimes She said: 'You aren't getting into the car like that, Biddy,' and then She would drive the car slowly along the short dead-end road with Biddy galloping beside it to get her coat dry. I didn't join in this silly game, but sat where I was and waited while the car came slowly back. The Major always waited too, till we all went past, waving to him, I think he would have liked to come in and swim, but of course couldn't do anything like that any more.

I can remember the long grass of that field particularly, because Biddy looked so beautiful leaping through it towards the water. I can leap perfectly well if I want to, but I wasn't going to compete, and plodded along behind. I wouldn't have done anything on purpose to hurt Biddy. I wouldn't have done that.

Behind our cottage was a wild place, full of bog and patches of gorse where there were always dry sticks for firewood, and rabbit holes. We used to go there almost every day and She would stoop down and collect wood and Biddy and I would explore. There wasn't anyone else to be met with there and even the farmer didn't come up; one day She told me he said he hadn't been there for twenty years. There were piles of stones which had once been drystone dykes and a cobbler's cottage, and we used to scramble about on them and go on and up to where a hill rose behind. One day we chased a hare – I went too – and knowing those idiots of animals I didn't get too excited; it would always come back to the beginning, as already stated. But Biddy got very excited indeed and chased and chased it. I followed her for a bit but this particular hare was cunning; he ran in a circle, but made it a wider and wider circle. Soon we were in a part of the moor I'd never seen or smelt before and She was left far behind, with Her firewood. I began to want to go back; it wasn't only because I never go far, but I smelt danger. I didn't know how it would show itself or what it was, but it was there. There were fewer rabbit holes and suddenly when she saw a deep hole, Biddy dived in. The hare had gone long ago and we'd lost him; I tried to warn Biddy but the fool hadn't the sense to come back out. Later she couldn't; it was a fox's hole, among the gorse, well hidden, wide and deep. I heard Biddy scream, the way she had when she first saw me, and I turned and ran back quickly. I knew there was nothing I could do for Biddy. There must have been a vixen in there with cubs, and a fox bites its victim through the throat. I ran and ran and in due course came back to where She was still picking up old pallid gorse wood for the fire. 'Hello, Alice,' She said. 'Where's Biddy? I expect she went further than you did.'

Biddy certainly had. There was no way in which I could tell Her, and anyway it was too late. We went back to the house with the bundled firewood and every so often She would go out and call: 'Biddy, Biddy,' but of course there was no answer. When it began to get dark She grew anxious. She kept going out and calling and searching and waiting; then at last She went to bed and left the front door open so that Biddy could come in. Next day She walked all over the field again calling and calling, and then She telephoned the Major and asked if he had seen or heard anything, because whenever anything happened anywhere he always heard of it first. But there was no news, although She rang up all the farms round about. It wasn't the time of year for lambs so there would have been no reason to shoot Biddy, who in any case didn't chase sheep. Presently the Major came up in his chair, with the Alsatian. 'Open the gate into the back field,' he said, 'and we'll see if Heidi can find her, because Heidi loved Biddy.' We opened the field gate and the Major drove his electric chair all over the bumps and hollows, and kept saying to Heidi: 'Find Alice,' because, as he said to Her, a dog's mind can only take in one thing at a time and they had always said they were coming to see

Alice whenever he drove up. But it was no good, as I knew; Heidi wouldn't leave the Major for long, as she'd been trained to stay near and guard him. She kept coming back and wagging her tail, and I tried to tell her it was all useless, but we weren't on the same wavelength. 'I've never been up here before in my life,' said the Major, who had lived in that part of the country always, before he went off to the Army training college at Woolwich in the years before the war.

It was very sad; during the days that followed we walked and searched and called, and the Major asked all the farmers all over again, and She advertised in the local newspaper for a large black missing poodle lost on the moor, answering to Biddy. Then someone said Biddy might have been stolen and taken away in a car, and that was the worst time of all for Her. 'If only I knew she was dead,' She kept saying. 'It wouldn't be so bad if I knew.' And I looked and looked at her and couldn't say a word. The only thing to do was to be patient, and I tried not to make any trouble I could help. The police and the R.S.P.C.A. rang up more than once, and She rang them, and for a long time everybody kept looking out, even on the motorways, and telling Her they hadn't seen anything like a large black poodle, and I knew they couldn't, because Biddy was dead and the fox would have eaten what was left of her, so there was nothing to find. I didn't feel as guilty as I would have felt if it had been my fault, but it was bad enough. I did wish I could have explained with my ears that it was no good going on looking and putting notices in the papers.

At last – it was a long time – She said to me one day very sadly: 'Well, Alice, it looks as though you're all I've got left,' and I began to be happy, but didn't do my extra special pirouette of joy when I can spin in the air, because it wasn't that sort of occasion.

So I was the Only Dog again.

What happened next was something She and I thought very funny, but no doubt we have an improper sense of humour.

The cottage was within driving distance of two towns, a large and a small. The larger town has different kinds of churches, Baptists and Holy Rollers and Presbyterians and Catholics and Episcopalians. I will say everyone gets on with everyone else quite well. Once a new clergyman came to the Episcopal Church and his name was the Reverend Herbert Dewey, B.A., so of course everyone called him Dewy Herb, though not to his face. Dewy Herb had an old mother he took care of and propped up with cushions and things; but if you ask me she will last longer than he does as she eats like a horse and sits there like Buddha, while Dewy Herb rushes about doing those things he ought to do. He was a small man with a tuft of dark hair on top of his head which he plastered sideways over the bald bit. All the unmarried and widowed ladies of the parish were after him except Her, and wherever Dewy went he was followed and chatted about and one woman came all the way from Brighton simply to live near him. Well, one afternoon it was opening day for somebody's garden with the proceeds to be given to the local hospital. That is done everywhere there in summer and it is a good idea, because they let me come too. This time, it was a particularly fine day and everybody was there, including us, and we walked about the garden and looked at the flowers which were all tidy and neat and then She said with truth that I wouldn't do any good to the velvet lawn, so we went towards the wild part which is in a wood and quite large. Sure enough along came Dewy Herb with his dog, which was young like I still was then, and a bit frisky about coming back when called. I *never* come back when called; She has to walk in the opposite direction and then I follow. Anyway, She and Dewy Herb fell into polite talk and he said: 'Let's go in and let them off the lead,' so we all trooped into the wood and I looked out of the corner of my eye and saw a crowd of women staring after us. The wood was an exciting place, being divided into two high slopes with a valley between, and in one place the former owner, a major-general, is buried with his wife in a high stone tomb with four spaniels buried north, south, east and west of them. I could still smell the spaniels' bones, but the retriever couldn't because she was too silly, and there were brambles all over the place and she sniffed at those instead. As for Her, She was getting stuck in the brambles and let me off the lead for a bit of peace. Dewy Herb did the same with his retriever. 'Don't go too far, Alice,' She said to me pointedly, so to tease Her I went as far as possible for me, which is still within sight. In fact the retriever and I scampered in different directions because we knew we didn't have much in common, and we hunted and rooted about for whatever it is dogs expect to find in brambles, and I capered a bit, and She and Dewy Herb began to call us back but we didn't come. In the end She climbed up the slope and tried to catch me and laddered Her tights, and then She chased me and didn't catch me for a long time, up and down; it was good fun. The retriever had got the idea and was doing the same for Dewy Herb, and in the end he took off his black coat and chased the dog in his shirt-sleeves. Afterwards they both caught both of us. All this had taken quite a long time and Dewy Herb was looking hot and bothered and not like a clergyman any more. When we all came out of the wood at last I saw the women looking at their watches, but didn't think any more about it at the time and neither did She.

Next day was Monday and we were shopping at the little grocer's at the top of town. Sure enough we met Dewy Herb again, but he was not pleased to see us one bit, and scuttled off like a rabbit; I almost chased him. She got the groceries and we went home.

Later that same day the Major came up. He wasn't in his electric chair, but in his great dark blue gleaming Bentley which he used on special occasions like going to the races, but it wasn't race day and it was the first time he had ever come up our road in it. He let down the window and said with a deep, bitter look in his blue eyes: 'I hear I have to congratulate you.'

'What about?' She was drinking gin as She hadn't expected him and had Her glass in one hand but didn't offer him any because he never drank nowadays. He still looked grim and didn't smile.

'Your engagement to Herbert Dewey.' It was evident that he had heard the story all wrong and so probably had everyone else; it is a great place for gossip. That was why Dewy Herb had run away at the shop.

'*That* silly little man?' She said, and started to laugh. Presently he joined in and I could tell that he was pleased because in the days when he could walk, in the Army, he had been six foot two in his socks. 'Everybody's talking about it,' he said. 'You went into a wood with him and were there for ages.'

'We were exercising our dogs, or rather they were exercising us, Alice, this is your fault. Really this place is the limit. No wonder poor Dewy looked scared this morning at the grocer's. I'll have to write him a letter telling him not to worry.' She was still laughing and so was he, and I biffed upwards with my nose and spilt gin all over Her jersey. 'Clowns,' said the Major with relief, looking at me and referring to the breed in general. It is true that he never now drank gin or whisky or anything of that kind, because at first, during the war when he was told he would never walk again and his Army career was finished, he took to drinking too much, and decided it would have to stop. It was like him to stop at once. That was why She hadn't offered him a drink, though most times he took a cup of tea.

'Bother you,' She said to me, and went into the garage to put the spilled glass down and brush Herself so that drops of gin fell all over the floor. I licked them up. I like gin and beer and whisky as well as sherry. It wouldn't take much to turn me into an alcoholic.

But it was true about the rumours and as soon as the Major had gone away She sat down and wrote a letter to Dewy Herb making a funny story of it and saying she wouldn't be any use to marry as she wouldn't polish the furniture, which was true. *I like to live by myself and so probably do you*, the letter ended. *Give my best regards to your mother.*

Soon a letter came back from Dewy. *I have laughed and laughed ever since getting your letter.* He was too polite to say that it was with relief. *The gossip in town rather unnerved me and I hoped you hadn't heard it and made myself scarce. God bless you. Always, Herbert.*

Shortly after that he went somewhere else and took his mother with him, and they say one day he will become a bishop.

We went on in this way, just being happy, for a bit. Of course there were the usual troubles a dog gets, like worms. I don't get tapeworms because dogs mostly get them from eating rabbits, and I have never managed to catch a rabbit. Roundworms on the other hand everybody gets, that is if you are talking about a dog. Any old house – our cottage was two hundred years old – is surrounded with their eggs in the soil, and I suppose I must have nosed at it and got them, and the worms grew inside me for quite a while. Roundworms have no personality and just lie around in the bile duct, She tells me, and the vet said not to worry as all dogs got them in the early years and later they would pass off of their own accord. He also said that if She saw me eating grass or gravel not to worry either as it was a natural cure. Now and again I would pass worms and She swooped on them with a piece of paper and had them burned, as otherwise they would have laid more eggs and started the whole business all over again. They didn't look at all interesting and I am glad to say I have no more nowadays.

There were other things like that, which you can't avoid no matter how clean you are, and I clean myself all over like a cat. I wasn't troubled with ticks – poor Biddy used to get them in her long fur in summer, because they dropped from the sheep – but every summer I had lice, especially round my ears and over my face, which was very undignified. She got rid of them with a tooth comb. They aren't the same lice as humans get, which is fortunate.

I love a good brush every day, even though my coat is short. She has a brush with wires at one end and bristles on the other one for the back and one for the stomach and head. When I see the brush coming I roll over and wait for it, or crouch down and wag my tail. Apart from all that my nose was coming on nicely and it was almost black. I hadn't much to complain about, and that always means that something is going to happen. That is life.

Apart from the goat women who had now gone away, nobody much lived in the farmhouse at the top of the road. It kept changing hands as it was not a very good farm, being mostly moor. Sometimes we had to stay inside because sheep were coming down to be dipped at the larger farm near the beginning of the road, but mostly it was quiet, and cars, like Ken and Mary had come up in, were rarely seen.

Then somebody else bought the farm at the top. They started by asking everybody to help them pay for having our road tarred so that bigger hay lorries could come up. I knew from the beginning that She wasn't pleased with the idea at all. 'I came to live up here for peace and quiet,' She said. 'If they tar the road we'll have courting couples coming up in cars and men on motor-bikes and lorries and everything else. It won't be the same any more.'

None of the other neighbours wanted the road tarred either, so the people at the top had to pay for it themselves. This put the new people in a bad temper with the lot of us and it showed itself in various ways. For instance the people had a fat daughter who walked up the road from school every day although she was driven down early each morning. I was usually about at that time in the afternoon and when she went past I didn't bark, just stood there looking down my nose. One day She and the Major were sitting chatting at our gate and I was out, and I forget where the Alsatian was. The schoolgirl – she was very fat indeed and had two pounds of pocket money a week to spend on sweets, which made it worse – began to yell about me.

'Ah'm sick to death of yon dog, Ah'm tellin' ye.' She wasn't a very nice girl. I went on looking down my nose and She called out from where She was sitting. 'The dog's not doing you any harm,' She said, which was true. The Major lit another cigarette in the ivory holder and listened.

'Ah'll get the police, Ah wull.'

'You do that,' She said cheerfully, and followed it up with a remark which wasn't very polite. The Major started to laugh and soon went home. I saw the new people's car whiz past and went in and found Her already on the telephone. She was talking to the local policeman at the station in Wigtown. He said it was quite all right about me as long as I didn't cause any damage or bite anyone. 'She doesn't bite them, but she might bulldoze them,' She said, which is true; sometimes in playing with Her I have almost broken Her nose.

At that point the Major rang up from his own house. 'I saw them drive down all together, looking like blue murder,' he said. But the police evidently told them the same thing as they had told Her and nothing more happened.

The road was treated first with weed-killer which is poisonous, so She wouldn't let me go out of the garden. Then they began to roll tar on it and nobody could get back and forth for shopping till the tar was dry. We learnt later that the contractor had cheated over the tar and had only laid it down half as thick as he was supposed to, with the result that it soon cracked and anyway the grass ribbon began to grow through again; you can't stop grass. Meantime our peace was destroyed in several ways, in addition to being on bad terms with a neighbour, which is never a good idea. Enormous lorries piled with hay began to come, and a pig van, and salesmen's cars, and the lorry drivers complained because their roofs hit the trees which had always been there and which overhung the road and made it look interesting, even now. So the new people at the top started to cut down the trees. A pretty crab apple which had stood at the top corner of the road was hacked away; we would never see its pink blossom in spring again. Worse than that, we ourselves had a very beautiful old elm, at least as old as the cottage. In the summer bees would hum in it all the time when the sun shone, getting honey from the small green flowers. It was a tree we liked to sit under. Unfortunately it had one long branch which overhung the road. This, She knew, would have to come down. 'But they aren't cutting down the whole tree, I'll see to that,' She said, and meant it, but an unexpected thing happened; just when the tree-cutters were getting to our part of the road with their circular saw, She had an anguished telephone call from the Major. He had been stopped for speeding in his hand-controlled Bentley, and wanted Her to type a letter for him at once to the Chief Constable to explain, as if lost his licence life wouldn't be worth living. It had to go off by the first post, so She dropped everything and drove down with Her portable typewriter to the Major's house not far away. She said afterwards She would have mailed the letter for him after it was written, but he wanted to do it himself. It had to be done at Dumfries, which was an hour and a half's drive away, or perhaps less in a Bentley. 'Anyway, don't get copped for speeding,' She said to him, and off he went with the letter. As soon as the Bentley had rounded the corner She got back into our car and hurried back up home; before She left She had spoken firmly to the man with the saw about only taking the overhanging branch, not on any account the tree. He had promised, but when we got back the first thing we saw was a huge greeny-white circle of sawn-off trunk close to the ground. The woman from the top had come down and insisted that the whole thing be cut to the base, which she had no right to do as it was on our ground. No doubt she did it out of spite because of not having been able to get help from the police about my standing in the road looking down my nose, and other reasons.

I could see that She was very sad and angry. It was something the same as when the mouse had eaten Balthasar's face, only worse: a needle and thread wouldn't put the tree back, nothing would. She wrote to Her lawyer and also got a man who called himself a tree surgeon, but all he did was look, in fact it was all anybody could do, and he said it would take thirty years to begin to look like a tree again. In the meantime the cottage was much colder, because the elm tree had sheltered it from that side. It hadn't been a diseased tree like some elms are; the disease hadn't reached our part of the country.

So things went on, with feelings growing worse

and worse, and in the end the people at the top gave up farming, because it wasn't paying, and started a caravan park instead. This was worse still because caravans used to rattle up and down all day and all night, and usually stopped at our door to ask if they were going the right way, so that in the end She put a notice telling them to keep right on. But the caravans that didn't stop were worse, as they drove so fast, and She had to come with me every time I went out, which I hadn't been used to, apart from our walks. The road was too narrow to take more than one caravan at once and we used to wonder what would happen if two tried to pass each other at the same time, but for some reason they never did.

This brings me to the next bit. Summer of course is the time for caravans, and so there was very little peace and quiet then. But as winter drew on things were quieter, and She heard that the people were thinking of giving up altogether as they didn't have enough of a water supply to support all those caravans one way and another. About November the trade stopped dead, and She decided it was safe for me to go out again alone, especially as I was sensible with cars.

So I was mooching about, when what had happened before happened again, and I was run over. This time it was my left hind leg which was broken, and they put in a metal shaft and for a long time it was set in plaster and I felt like an elephant and tried to scratch the plaster off. At least now I was symmetrical, so to speak, with two metal legs on the same side.

It wasn't a car which had run me over and it wasn't a caravan: the curious thing was that it was an AA van with the driver inside going fast because he was going home; he and his wife – they were quite young – were living in one of the caravans for the winter because they had nowhere else to go. He was a nice AA driver and stopped when I was hurt and apologised, and kept coming back daily to ask how I was, which is more than the last one had done. One day I found Her looking at Herself in the glass.

'Alice,' She said, 'I'm getting old and boring and our luck here is running out, for the time being at any rate.' She could hardly bear to go past the place where the elm tree had been cut down, and She got difficult and mopey with one thing and another. 'Let's go to London for six months,' She said, 'and let's ask that nice AA man and his wife if they'd like to live here over the winter: it must be very cold just now in a caravan.'

She asked the AA man and he almost jumped for joy and promised that at the end of the six months they would move out. One had to be careful about that kind of thing. As for us, we drove down to Her London flat which She had been letting furnished to make up for the money She didn't earn from Her books when there hadn't been enough peace to write them.

* * *

By that time I was slightly different. In recent months I had been a bit depressed, which is not like me. It had happened most of all when She played the piano. She wasn't much good and I used to howl and dive down between the pedals just as I had done in the car when we came to a cattle grid. 'There is evidently no future,' She said at last, 'in keeping this piano. A friend told me it ought to be like a Mighty Wurlitzer and sink through the floor to leave room for company,' so She sold it and used the money to help us stay in London. But as regards myself and my troubles, I had been licking at myself a great deal and although She sometimes said: 'Stop licking' in an absent-minded sort of way, She didn't bother about why I was doing it. It was only when I was under an anaesthetic on the operating table while having a plaster like a Wellington boot put on my broken hind leg that the vet noticed I had a discharge which must have been going on for some time. I had been licking it away to keep tidy, but while I was out for the count they couldn't help noticing it. She was waiting outside and the vet went out and said to Her that it would be best at the same time to perform an operation on my inside which is called a hysterectomy. She was very sad – it meant I wouldn't go into season any more and couldn't have any more puppies – but She said of course if it was necessary it would have to be done. So they cut out quite a bit of my inside, the bag that holds the puppies before they are born and the ovaries which start the whole thing off, then stitched me up and when I was coming round on the floor I heard them say they'd never had a dog on the table before for plaster and an operation as well.

When I came round completely I was in Her car and feeling fairly rotten. When we got home She laid me on Her bed just as She had done when I was having the puppies. Then She said: 'Well, Alice, it's only you and me from now on, and we're going to enjoy ourselves in London.'

She brought a photograph to show me that had come in with the mail. It was of Her and me and the elm tree and it had been taken some time before by a photographer, because Her publishers had written to ask if She could have an up-to-date one taken as the old one on the back of Her books didn't tell the truth any more. The photograph of me was quite good except that I had laid my ears back, not knowing the photographer from Adam. It cheered me up and She stroked me and told me to go back to sleep, and I went.

I can't remember how we got to London, but we did get there, and I was out of plaster and able to climb down the steep flight of steps that led to the basement flat. At first when you went in there was a long dark passage, then a sunny room on the left where She was going to work, and a few more dark places again and then a French window and a nice paved garden with a fig tree leaning over from next door. That cheered things up and so did being able to walk to the shops. There was a market too, where they sell all kinds of peculiar fish we hadn't heard of in Scotland. There were plant and vegetable stalls as well, with cabbages and big fat melons and marrows, and little tight bunches of rosebuds, very expensive. Everybody had a dog. I made friends with a ghost dog called Henry who belonged to some glass merchants. It wouldn't have mattered if he had looked in a mirror because he couldn't have seen himself; he was a pale grey colour and very thin, but knowledgeable. There were cats too. I don't know why I have to chase cats. I think these were the first I had seen, and like the rabbits they were faster than I was. Once I did get a ginger tom-cat into a corner and chased him down our basement steps, and the door was open and he went inside and sat in the hall, then suddenly turned round and began boxing with me, quite amiably, with his paws. I let him go in the end. One reason for so many cats is that a woman round the corner fed strays every night with meat. They came slinking along like anything then, but She wouldn't let me out. However I got my own back in the garden: sometimes cats would appear at the lattice which is the boundary, and I would go roaring over the flowerbeds and hurl myself at the cat, or rather at the place where it had been, and bricks from the flowerbed, which were loose just there,

would come rattling down and She would have to put them up again, until the next cat came. They also had the gall to sun themselves on the garden steps, or would have if it had been summer. They never arrived when they were likely to meet me, but whisked out of the way as soon as an engagement offered. It upset my dignity slightly not to catch them, but I consoled myself with the thought that I am not the slowest moving of dogs; a St Bernard is slower, and Alsatians – the Major had told us this already – have only two speeds, like a bicycle; they walk or else they lope. I have at least three kinds of quickness; the Plod, the Run, the Charge and, as I have already described, the Upward Plunge. This last can happen at any time unexpectedly, like when I knocked over Her gin or when stupid people make swiping movements to try and fend me off. I refuse to be fended. They don't make the gesture twice. I have a jaw that can pound anything to powder and a nose that can hit anything unconscious and if anyone tries to hit me back they hurt themselves, not me. I remember when I was a puppy She gave it up as a bad job and had recourse to a wooden spoon when I needed chastising, which wasn't often or very hard, but I still pretend to be frightened when She raises it even though She doesn't use it any more. In fact She only had to say 'Spoon' to make me pipe down.

The Charge needs preparation; it is special. It ties in with the fact that when She calls me I go in the opposite direction. She understands my principles quite well and if She is in a hurry walks on and knows I will follow in my own good time. If She is not in a hurry, and we are in a place where it doesn't matter, like gardens and graveyards, She turns round and crouches down and holds out Her hands and whistles. Then I go into the Charge which is done at terrific speed, like cavalry, with my head lowered like a bull. Nervous people think they are going to be hit, but She knows I have it worked out to the last inch and skid to a halt with my ears pricked devilwise. In fact not many people apart from Her ever see it. As for the very special pirouette of joy, that is only for Her and when I do the spin I am airborne for an instant, like Nijinsky whom She said I resembled in such ways. He was a very famous ballet dancer who they say could actually stay poised for a split second in the air, but it was probably what drove him mad. I only go mad on purpose, not by accident, and at all other times remain as sane as a whistle. I would be aware of this even if She hadn't told me so.

She and the Major had telephoned often and written to each other even though he didn't write easily because the muscles in his hands had gone. I knew that part of the reason why we had come to London was to try to find some different news to entertain him, because up there there only seemed to be what he'd heard already. He liked news and gossip and took great delight in hearing it first before anyone else so that he could spread it all over the place. However he wrote that he missed Her and missed me, and She kept the letters in Her jewel case in their envelopes.

Once he asked Her to try to find a special colour of cellular blanket for him, as it was winter up there and cold. It had to be olive green, because that was the one he had had for years and it was all in holes, and no other colour would do. She and I went to all sorts of shops looking for exactly such a blanket, and they had them in peach and they had them in pink and white and lilac and pale blue and yellow, but never olive green. In the end She found the right one in Harrods. I remember that visit particularly because when we were in the lift going up to the proper department the man who pushed buttons said: 'Can't bring that dog in 'ere. Can't bring a dog into 'arrods.' I believe this is now true, but it wasn't then, and she copied me and looked down Her nose (She is taller than the lift man was) and said: 'Since when?' and he had to admit that it had only been decided some weeks before, and later a nice lady assistant, who produced the blanket at last, explained that it was because dogs get mixed up in moving staircases. This is fair enough and I wouldn't like it to happen to myself. Anyway we got the right blanket. Unfortunately She didn't send it by post but by delivery, and delivery took three months, which meant winter was almost over. By this time we were going back to Scotland anyway and might as well have brought it up ourselves.

There is more about London but I will explain all that later on.

Five

One day spring appeared and we went back to the cottage, which the AA man and his wife had left shining and clean, more than She ever bothered to do. The very next day the Major appeared in his car for news, carrying a huge bunch of daffodils and narcissus. She was pleased and said she'd put them in water right away, and while She was inside doing that the Major talked to me and said I was getting fat and lazy. She came out again and got into the car and they talked for a long time. There was one more visit, in a few days, when he came up in the old way with the electric chair and the Alsatian. She was getting ready for a cocktail party somewhere and after a bit said She would have to go and get dressed. 'What you've got on is perfectly all right,' he said, 'won't it do?'

'Of course not,' She said, and I knew afterwards that they were words She regretted very much. We both watched the chair and the Alsatian going back down the road and didn't know it was for the very last time.

Two days later – it was only two – it snowed. I don't much care for snow as it is only rain disguised. Poor Biddy used to love it and come in with great balls of white stuff collected round her legs and feet. Anyway, the snow was coming down and there was a knock at the door. She went to open it and there was the farmer's wife from down the road, with her bicycle. She stood in the snow and said: 'I had to come up when I heard the news.' She had blue eyes like the Major, and they were troubled.

'What's happened?' She said. 'Come in.'

'Then you haven't heard. Oh, my dear, he's dead.' We all knew he meant the Major; it couldn't have been anyone else.

She didn't start crying; She stood quite still and said: 'Come in,' again, and the farmer's wife came inside and told us more about it; she'd heard over the telephone. The Major had gone to sleep the night before with his dog beside him in his room, on the floor, as usual, and the telephone by his bedside. In the morning his man had found him dead of heart failure, with his hand on the telephone trying to call the doctor. When the door was opened the Alsatian ran out of the house and wouldn't go back. Dogs know quite well when the person isn't there any more.

She went to the telephone then and began to call up all sorts of people, like a clockwork doll which works when you wind it. It was mostly: 'I can't come to the party tonight, because, haven't you heard –' and then all sorts of other people started to ring Her up about it, and the farmer's wife sat there for a bit and then went quietly away. She thanked her for bringing up the news and let her go. It had stopped snowing.

As soon as She was alone She went away from the telephone and sat down and was very, very sad. I didn't go and lick Her hand or bother Her because when people are feeling like that all they want is to be left alone. After a while She came over to me and said, as She'd said after the operation and after Biddy vanished, 'Well, Alice, you really are all I've got now. I'm glad we came back from London in time.'

She had rung up the Major's housekeeper to ask if She might go down and see him. Then She went into the garden and poked among the snow and picked all the primroses there were, and took them down in a bunch. She went into the house without me and presently came back again without the primroses. The housekeeper had come out to see Her off and She said suddenly: 'What's going to happen to the dog?' and I was scared for a moment that She was going to offer to take the Alsatian, which would not have been a good idea. In the end the man who had looked after the Major kept it, and I saw it once some time afterwards and it had been turned into the kind of dog that gives a paw. I think it should have been allowed to go when the Major went, as he had always said he wanted to happen. However nobody asked me one way or the other.

We thought about him a lot, She and I. 'Do you know,' She said once, 'he told me he had that bull terrier called Tony just before the war, and Tony had been so naughty all his life no one could do anything with him until he came to the Major, and then he would even climb mountains with him.' When the war came and the Major was to be sent overseas he had to have Tony put down as I said, and must have been very sad but he never talked about it. Once I was listening while he talked to Her and he was saying that when we die we don't go on anywhere, everything just stops, and She said: 'Nonsense. When you die the first thing you'll do is wake up afterwards and Tony will be there asking you to take him for a walk.' I hope it happened like that; in any case it must be wonderful for him to be able to get about again after all those years in an electric chair.

The Major's funeral was very plain, because he was a humanist and had left orders that there was to be no service and no singing. He was cremated and afterwards they scattered his ashes in the places he'd loved best. In a few days She had prayers said for him in Her own church and a lot of people were there, and the organist played *Who Would True Valour See*, because of the Major.

When we were driving home afterwards She said to me: 'Do you know, Alice, that if it hadn't been for him I would never have got you at all? He almost dared me to take on a bull terrier. He said I'd never control one, and I probably don't control you, but I like you as you are.'

In a way She was right and in a way She was wrong. I would do anything for Her, within reason, but I must say I like to do things my own way best.

The snow started again and was nearly as bad as one year when we'd been snowed up at the cottage and the postman couldn't get up the road and the hills were covered with a white veil and we had to live out of tins. We had condensed milk as well which I like, and She made Her own bread and my biscuits. It was fun while it lasted. If I had to go out, which didn't happen oftener than necessary, I used to clean my feet like a cat as I always do if they happen to get wet. The snow went away in the end and then gradually it was summer, and I could see She was getting tired of living at the cottage now the Major wasn't there any more. One day She said to me 'Alice, I've never really liked it here since they cut the elm tree down. Let's sell it and go and live in London for good. It's the only place for a writer.'

That was all very well, but I knew it wasn't the best place for a dog. I hoped She would change Her mind, but meantime She went about saying goodbye to everybody, including a very interesting cousin of the Major's who lived about thirty miles off and had been a prisoner of war, and after returning home had collected all kinds of animals who were in danger of extinction.

He lived with his wife in a large grey house behind which were woods, and in the woods he had once kept a wild pig called Fred. I will relate the story of Fred, which is sad, in due course, but meantime the Major had told us once that in the drawing room, there was a goat sitting on the sofa. By that time the goat was dead, which was a pity, but outside there were all kinds of unusual things; Silkie hens, a Clydesdale horse called Bernadette and a number of white peacocks. They were a bit worried about me and asked if I would chase anything, but I didn't. I had seen superior peacocks in all sorts of different colours in a garden She had once taken me to in Sussex, and they were displaying, which means spreading their gorgeous feathers out like a fan and wiggling their terra-cotta backsides, and all for the sake of one plain little peahen who didn't seem in the least interested. It takes all sorts. Anyway the white peacocks left me cold, but I was amused when some Eriskay ponies began to bite Her in the small of the back, which is their way of introducing themselves.

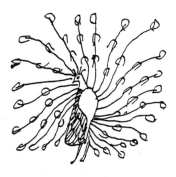

These ponies were so nearly extinct that there were only three of them left at last on an island in the Hebrides, two mares and a gelding. There didn't seem much hope for the breed at that rate, but the Major's cousin decided to take them anyway, and when he brought them back to the mainland discovered both mares were in foal; whoever had done the gelding hadn't made a proper job of it. The foals grew up and multiplied, and by the time of which I write the breed was becoming very popular for carriage-racing, so the whole thing is a success story.

So, in his way and while it lasted, was Fred. The Major's cousin had sent for a pair of Ancient British wild pigs, of a kind which used to roam the ancient forests and live on acorns, and there were plenty of acorns in his woods. The sow and boar arived, and next day squeaks came from the hut where they'd been put as they didn't, like the late goat, live in the

87

drawing-room. There was a handsome litter, striped, and all of them were given names. One was Fred. Soon he and the rest were rooting about for their own acorns and the sow was making ready to litter again, because sows have a habit of it.

Unfortunately the neighbours grew nervous. They hadn't minded anything much previously except the goat, because goats strip the bark off trees. Nevertheless an ancient British boar can be an unnerving sight if anyone is inclined that way, although it is perfectly sociable and likes having its back scratched like any other pig. It has enormous curly tusks and a little red eye that looks angry but isn't. It is, of course, accustomed to roaming free and takes no notice whatever of barriers, and can accordingly be found eating the neighbours' geraniums and other such items.

Very reluctantly, the Major's cousin was persuaded to shoot the lot. On counting the corpses, it was found that Fred had not turned up for roll-call and was still alive somewhere in the woods.

In all the circumstances, nobody could be blamed for wishing Fred luck. He had an astonishing faculty for managing not to be seen. He survived in the woods for quite a long time, then when love called – it always calls sooner or later – he began to venture further afield. He was simply never seen by day, and made his way past ruined castles and woods full of bluebells and fields and even high roads to where there were valuable Middle White sows on a well-known pig farm. In the intervals of courtship, Fred would go down to the local pub, always at night. He used to be seen crossing the bridge just at closing time, and many of those coming out never touched a drop again, or so it is said, as they thought they were seeing things. Fred by this time was extremely large and his tusks resembled an orchestral tuba.

Meantime, his prowess had got into the local papers, especially as most of the litters born that season, and the next, were striped. The farmers were furious, and formed a league to finish Fred off, but he kept them guessing for a very long time, like the Scarlet Pimpernel. Bets were placed and the public began to take a great interest and if they were not farmers, were mostly on Fred's side. It began to be rumoured that he had mated all the sows in the West of Scotland and that the price of bacon was rising because none of the litters could be brought on.

They got him in the end, of course, by a trick; they put a not particularly valuable sow out to lure him, and waited with their guns. Fred came along out of hiding, trotting along on his delicate little hooves, and the farmers fired all the lead they had into him. He ran for 120 yards, pouring blood, then dropped. There was an obituary in the papers.

When She heard the story She was so sympathetic about Fred that She gave a dinner party at the cottage and invited the Major's cousin and his wife and some other people and we all ate not pork, but shepherd's pie. That happened shortly before the cottage was sold.

It was quite easy to sell it, and in fact two people who were on a walking tour bought it almost at once, for a great deal more than She had paid for it. She started to pack up and on the night before we left, She gave me a bath so that I would look respectable where we were going next. As soon as She had dried me – I hate having baths – I went out to the road and rolled in the tar and then went into the field and rolled in a cowpat, and came back covered in all that and dust as well. It was a form of protest. I will say She took it very well and laughed for almost the first time since the Major had died, and didn't even bring out the wooden spoon. 'Perhaps people will think you're a brindle,' She said. 'I only hope they don't take a deep breath.'

The removal itself was good fun. There is a man called Mr Dill who lives in Wigtown and used to grow mushrooms for a living but found that removing paid better. He has an Irish assistant named Hughie who is six feet four inches tall and very thin, like a rake, and in summer he wears a daisy chain round his head and in winter a small string of beads. Nor is this all, because as he works and gets hotter and hotter he strips off more and more patterned knitted pullovers, and after the last one has come off and Hughie is only in his trousers he looks very spectacular, because there is a girl on a flying trapeze tattooed in bright blue across his chest. It was sad to see the furniture going out of the cottage and in the end She walked straight out without saying goodbye, and didn't look back.

If this had been a properly conducted story we would have gone south immediately, but some time before, She had noticed a derelict house in Wigtown which must have been there all the time, but She had never bothered to look at it previously. Now it was decided that we were going there instead, at least in the meantime.

Wigtown is quite a small place despite being the county town, and as a rule people mostly go there because it has a good butcher who has made so much money he can fly an aeroplane of his own at weekends. Otherwise there is one day in the year when Wigtown is the hub of the universe and that is the day of the Show. The Show is held in a field and there are pens and rings full of wonderful cattle and horses that have been brought from all over the country, and there is not a single place in the streets to park, and our farmer below the cottage always wins cups and prizes for his Galloway bulls whether I happen to have chased them or not.

But for the rest of the year Wigtown is quiet. I got to know its pavements quite well and some of them are made with patterns left over from the days when Wigtown was a very important place and old prints show it with ships sailing up into the harbour. There wasn't a harbour left for a great many years as it got silted up with mud, and She used to take me down there and I would gallop through the mud and have a mud bath, which is a very pleasant feeling, nearly as good as rolling in cowpats in the fields at home. However some people in Wigtown thought it would be a good idea to have a harbour again and they all went out and dug till the water came in, and shored up the banks with old cars filled with clay. There was a walk down to the harbour and we used to meet the doctor with his dogs there, as he went every day. He used to breed pointers but they must have got out, as nearly all the dogs in Wigtown now have peppered brown spots in one place or other. It was rather like Fred. By the time we got there the doctor had given up the pointers and now he has spaniels, who are dogs of no discretion and make friends with everybody. I do not, because I am a car and house guard and so earn my keep. Nobody dares to open the car door when I am inside it but Her, and although we have never yet had burglars I will stand foursquare to meet them and give them short shrift when they come. Not everyone realises this. Once She left the car with me in it and also the keys, and a policeman with a nice face came up and said: 'Madam, you've left the keys in your car,' and She said: 'There's a bull terrier in my car as well.' He tried to persuade her that anybody could come along and give me a bit of meat and put me off guard, but this will not happen. Anyway She removed the keys because it is better not to argue with the police. I will now return to the matter of the derelict house.

It seems to be impossible for Her to see a derelict house without buying it and doing it up. She did it again later on. It is like the way some people feel about children. This house was in a sloping street that went down to the fields near the harbour and past the old church where there are supposed to be martyrs buried. The house had ugly yellow framed windows and a blue front door and half the slates were off and once you got inside, everything was dirty and depressing and painted a heavy cream colour which had turned yellow like the outside. At the back was a garden full of rubbish and an old tin shack. I must say that having seen it and smelt it I was not impressed, but She had noticed a sign above the door which said 1840, carved in stone, and the architect's initials. Now that She had made quite a lot of money from selling the cottage She went on letting the flat in London again for a bit and got on with buying the derelict house and finding workmen to do what She wanted to it. At the beginning there was a fight with the planning permission people who wanted everything left as it was while they argued about it at a meeting, because the house was what they call listed and of architectural interest, though it didn't look like it until She got started. By the end it had all its tiles on and two superb wide windows at the top, looking over the Solway estuary, and lots of different birds used to fly up and perch on the telephone lines outside. The planning people said we shouldn't have put in the windows without asking them, and She said we had but they were taking too long, and in the end She got away with it, which not everyone does. The outside of the house was cleaned up and the stones pointed and a damp course put in and new eight-paned windows, which looked much nicer, especially when they and the door were painted white. She had a brass dolphin put on the door for people to knock with, but of course they always used the bell. Inside, it was all painted light colours, and the bathroom was particularly grand with an avocado bath and a pink ceiling and matching pink tweed curtains which She had knitted on very large needles, quite quickly.

My life in Wigtown was slightly different from what it had been; for one thing if She ever let me out at the front door people said, at first: 'Is that white dog out?' and mothers used to pull their children away when I went past. Gradually they got used to me and She used to take me with her to the butcher's and I liked the smell so much that I used to head back there from wherever in the town She might be. It was more or less opposite where we lived so that was a good thing. Another place where I was quite at home was the garage, and everybody used to say: 'Hello, Alice,' when I went past. But there was one place I would never go past even when She was with me on walks, and that was the vet's house. I still remembered my operation although it had happened at the surgery, which was somewhere else. Bull terriers are supposed to have bad noses, but mine was good enough to tell me he drove up and down there every day, and I wasn't going to pass it, thank you very much all the same.

Best of all I liked it when She took me down the slope of the road, either for my mud bath or, on the days when I was clean, the patch of mown grass behind the church. The graveyard was next door and there was a notice saying NO DOGS and then two open spaces where an elephant could have got in, but the place we went to was beside that and nobody could see us from the road and I liked to go mad. It was just as though all the free times I had once had in the fields beside the cottage were lumped into one and I had to get on with it quickly, and I raced round and round in The Charge and skidded back to where She was waiting, and to this day if She says 'Alice come to graveyard' I know what it means and oblige as far as possible, depending on circumstances.

In the graveyard itself were the martyrs' graves

which are a tourist attraction, and quite a lot of cars stopped there in summer and Americans and other people got out. I happen to know She doesn't believe there were any martyrs at all because when at some point somebody tried to dig them up to see how they were getting on, they only found sheeps' bones, and many people claim the story was a put-up job and there have been books written about it, but not by Her. Two women, one old and one young, were said to have been tied to stakes and drowned in the Solway, more or less at the place where I took my mud bath, for not doing what they were told about religion. While we were living in Wigtown the martyrdom was three hundred years old and the whole thing was re-enacted while a bell tolled from the Town Hall which was said to be the same bell as then. All sorts of young girls were dressed up as the martyrs, in long skirts and shawls, and there was a procession and wreaths were laid, and it was all reported in the local paper. People can believe what they like nowadays which is a good thing, and nobody drowns them in this country whatever happens elsewhere.

All this time we were living in the restored house and it was very pleasant in many ways, but much too near everything for Her, and the front door bell and the telephone bell were always ringing and She couldn't get on with Her typing in peace; in fact I don't think She wrote anything at all while we lived in Wigtown, but this turned out to be only for a year. She put the house up for sale after the garden was more or less ready and She had had the tin shanty ripped down and the rubbish cleared by about fifty small boys who took it to the top of the hill where the martyr's monument is and it helped with the Fifth of November bonfire. Then She and two men who helped Her dug and divided the garden into two halves, one with raised crazy paving and the rest beds, and all sorts of flowers began to come up including a little heartsease like a tiny pansy, all over the place. Soon She had dug in a pond – there had been a small one at the cottage and the first thing I did when I was a puppy was fall in – and actually planted a water lily, but as soon as that was put in the Wigtown house was sold.

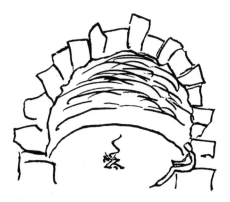

She has a habit of going mad when She thinks She is on to the right thing, and one day when we were driving with friends down to Isle of Whithorn, which is by the sea and a great many people keep boats there, She saw a ruin and got out to look. Inside was a very old arched stone fireplace and nothing else. She got excited and as the site was for sale, went and bought it and started to build a house round the fireplace, saying we would all make our fortunes once it was sold and I could live on sirloin steak. She hired an architect and he and She and I used to drive down to see how the building was getting on. Once the builder tried to put hardboard in front of the fireplace to hide it, as he wasn't very bright and neither was the architect, but She stopped them in time and said the fireplace was a feature and what did they think they were doing? She and the architect used to go and have lunch at a pub which made venison stew, but wouldn't let me in, and they used to come out again breathing venison, which was extremely tantalising.

When the house was built – it didn't take long, and ended up with a pleasant view of the bay – an odd thing had happened; the fireplace had looked quite small when there was nothing else there, but once it was inside it looked enormous, enough to roast an ox, but we didn't have any oxen. Even She knew it was going to take a great deal of fuel to keep fires going, and perhaps for that reason the house was slow to sell.

In the end Her lawyer wrote to say why didn't She put a few odds and ends of furniture in and let it for the summer? It would at least make some money in the meantime.

Being Her, She didn't put in just anything, but had every single thing made brand new out of polished pine; a round folding table, beds, chests, the lot, and all the curtains and covers were blue. They say dogs can't see colours and so I won't argue, but if She said things were blue they were blue, with frills and everything that was needed. However the house agent who came to arrange summer lettings didn't seem satisfied, and said we needed a great many more things including an ironing board and iron. 'Who wants to do ironing on a summer holiday?' She said, but he told Her people were queer, so She got the iron and everything including teaspoons. At the last minute before the tenants were due to move in, an offer came for sale. Life is like that.

The offer was from a bank manager, so we knew it was sound. He had sat beside the enormous fireplace and when asked how he would keep it going had replied dreamily 'Driftwood from the shore.' We knew he was going to be busy at that rate, but anyway the offer came in, and in Scotland it has to be settled one way or the other in twenty-four hours and after that nobody can wriggle out again. She accepted the offer, and didn't argue about whether the bank manager wanted the furniture or not, not to mention all the blue draperies and teaspoons. However the letting agent tore his hair and said he'd signed up leases with tenants, so She had to make it a condition of the sale that the lettings were allowed to take place first, which meant the bank manager wouldn't be collecting any driftwood till next year.

However he agreed, but worse happened, because the VAT people sent Her a bill for selling a business as a going concern, and although She sent a letter from the agent they wouldn't change their minds. In the end it cost Her as much as if She had never set eyes on the fireplace in the first instance, and She said to me it really was time we got away fast and went to London, and in the end we did.

Meantime I did a very expensive thing. When the house was being done up at first She had decided that it would be nice to have a greenhouse at the back, using up some of the garden ground where the corrugated iron shanty had been. Also She is very lazy and can't be bothered pulling out more weeds than necessary. She likes planting things, however. About the greenhouse, all sorts of permission had to be obtained because it was to lean against the house, whereas if it had been separate we could have gone ahead on our own. Men came and filled in all sorts of little forms She had to sign, then She employed an architect who got drunk and didn't come back, and She said She could do a drawing as well as anybody and did, and at last the permission – they call it a building warrant – was sent in spite of the argument about the upstairs windows with the view, and then a builder came who had magnificent National Helath Service teeth, the kind they call wallies in Scotland, and his name was Ernie. Ernie was terrified of me, so She kept me out of the way while the building of the greenhouse was going on, especially as there had to be a cement floor of a certain thickness according to the warrant, and if I had got in there while it was drying out my prints might have been seen in it for ever and ever or, worse, I might have got stuck in the cement likewise. However at last the greenhouse was ready for use and very pleasant it was, as the sun made it warm, and She put in all sorts of potted plants She had brought down from the cottage. As summer came on She would leave the back door open, so that it was one long run (The Charge) from the street through the front door down the passage through the greenhouse into the garden. At least, that is what it ought to have been.

Now, one day I was pottering about by the front door when I saw a cat. It was as simple as that. The cat was in the back garden and that was enough for me. I roared down the passage and through the back door and out into what ought to have been the garden and broad daylight, and there was an almighty sound of splintering glass and when I came to myself and shook it off She was shrieking at me and I had cut my nose and the plants were all knocked sideways, and the cat had gone.

I will say She doesn't fuss for long. She picked up the broken glass and put it out in a box for the dustman, and sent for Ernie again to put in new glass, and when he heard why he laughed and laughed and his wallies flashed in the sun. 'Told you you'd have to watch that dog,' he said. She merely asked if he could make the glass unbreakable this time, and he said he could but that it was very expensive and what about plastic? Meantime the house had got very cold and draughty because of what I'd done, and She told me I was a menace and said she wouldn't let me out of the back door unless the greenhouse door was open. 'Then you can get out and chase pink elephants if you want to,' She said. She was too tactful to remind me I hadn't caught the cat.

I really can't understand why people like Ernie are terrified of me. The man who bought the cottage was terrified too, and I believe as soon as they moved in they found a cat sitting outside waiting to be fed. It all goes to show what a good influence I am when I try; there hadn't been a cat seen up at the cottage for years.

I am by nature tactful. If She is typing I make no noise and simply go to sleep in the only comfortable armchair there is. When She stops typing She generally cooks or does knitting, or even reads a book. I let Her do all this in peace as long as I am offered bits left over from the cooking. That is only fair. The one thing we disagree about is rugs. She has a habit of making long woolly pile ones with a hook and canvas; they simply ask to be rumpled up as soon as they are finished. If I am annoyed or want Her attention drawn to anything I get on my back and roll the rugs right up into a ball, one after the other. She goes round the house after me putting them straight again and saying that if it wasn't for me they would never be shaken, but it gets a bit much if I do it again immediately. Once a very expensive white rug came back from the cleaners and I rolled and rolled on it till it was grey again, on purpose. 'I'll jolly well wash it in the bath next time and you too,' She said. However I am very clean now that we live in town and I don't even have summer lice any more.

They say a bull terrier is A Smart Companion For The Man About Town and by now, in my case at least, it is true, except that She is not a man.

When She isn't reading or knitting or typing or cooking she sometimes says that She must think about getting television and keeping up with events. However She tried it at the cottage and found it a bore and I howled like I did about the piano, and She used that as an excuse to send it back. There are some things I wish I'd seen; they tell me there was a bull terrier shown on the screen on a skateboard. I have never been on one of those and should like to try, but it isn't the sort of thing She gets at Her age, and probably my metal leg would not do either.

Sometimes, while She still had the car, we went to places. We went to see Ken and Mary's Bull Terrier Open Day in Humberside. All sorts of bull terriers from all over Britain were there with their owners, and people and dogs were sitting about on the shaved June grass and there were competitions of all kinds and dog fancy dress parades and although She did not show me or dress me up, which bull terriers don't in fact approve of any more than we do of sitting up and begging, we were able to walk about and meet the dogs who had come, and the ones who were bred there for sale, and a special sad place for the ones who had been found abandoned and had been brought here to be made better if it was possible and found new homes. They hadn't any expression on their faces, because a bull terrier doesn't have large goggling soulful eyes, and it is often difficult to tell what he is thinking about everything. I say 'he' on purpose because bitches aren't often abandoned as they are easier to deal with. But a dog is very independent, very strong-willed, and very powerful. There is a deadpan expression we can all put on to protect ourselves from the foolish curiosity, even cruelty, like Toughy had had to put up with. (Toughy was there and doing very well.) But seeing those abandoned dogs is a thing I can never forget. It was rather like seeing humans who are holding up a street corner or lying rolled in a blanket because they have no job and no home and nobody loves them, so they go deadpan too. Ken and Mary are very careful about who gets these dogs next time, although it costs something to keep and feed them. One wrong owner is bad enough, but a second would be worse. You have to be tough, and understanding, to manage a bull terrier and make him respect you, then he will begin to trust you if he decides you are all right. On the other hand if you think that because he shows no expression he is brainless, and take a swipe at him or kick him, he may very well knock your teeth out. I say this in case anyone who reads this story suddenly decides even by now, that they would like a bull terrier. Don't buy one unless you are perfectly sure you understand and can cope. It will be worth it if you can; they are all, every single one, characters and they will delight you and drive you to despair, or even make you want to roll on the floor on your back like they do themselves when they are happy. They are perfect company in this and all sorts of other ways, but they love once very much and if that love is betrayed they may never, never trust a second person again, or anyone. But some do seem to manage it, in spite of everything.

The answer is that we are not everybody's dog. Some people simply don't like us and that is that. Once I went with Her into a wine shop in London and a young man who was waiting said to me: 'Don't you come near me, you dog,' and She said: 'Don't be silly, she's on a lead and anyway won't touch you,' and then we went on to the newsagent's, and the girl behind the counter said with a sour look at me: 'I can't think why it's so friendly when it's got such a vicious face. I think it looks like a goat.' I remembered the time when everyone had said I was like a pig and one person I have mentioned even called me a doglet, but none of these people matter. 'Did you hear what she said?' She asked me that time, and everyone in the shop smiled except the assistant. It is the only way to handle such episodes; it isn't worth getting angry and starting a fight.

Often children get frightened too, just at the sight of me. However I remember one day before leaving Wigtown when we went for a walk past some council houses and a little boy came out and asked quietly if he could stroke me. That made up for a lot of things. I let him do as much stroking as he liked and then he put his arms round me and smiled with happiness. He was quite a little boy, perhaps five. That was pleasant, but a few days later another little boy was passing our door and he was on a tricycle, and I just happened to be let out then and he began to scream and cry, so I looked down my nose. I know some parents teach their children to be afraid of dogs, but if I were a child I wouldn't be taught. Take a cat, now; if it knows somebody can't stand cats it goes up and rubs itself against them, just to annoy. Dogs aren't like that. Some of course have been ill-treated and will bite, but it isn't their fault, it is the fault of the people who own them.

Some people are very cruel indeed to their dogs. Many farmers work their collies hard all day with the sheep and at night kick them under the table with only flaked maize to eat, and when they are past work they let them starve. Once at one of the farms near the old cottage there was a collie puppy called Meg, a little fluffy thing, and she was kept tied up to an apple tree so that she wouldn't run out on the road and get killed, and She used to call for milk there and always went to see Meg and rub her stomach and play with her. For some reason we didn't go back there for two years, and one day She called in and heard a thump, thumping noise, and there was Meg grown up and all muddy, wagging her tail. She went over and Meg rolled on her back and She had to rub her muddy stomach, and always did when we went again to that farm, but presently She began to worry about Meg because she was always muddy and never got dry, and was kept at night chained in a barrel among the tractor mud of the yard. 'She'll get rheumatism,' She said to the farm hand, 'and then she won't be able to work.' But he only grinned as though She was daft, and She didn't report it to the R.S.P.C.A. because they can only take action if a dog is not exercised or fed, and Meg was exercised all right and wasn't starving. So there was nothing to be done, and soon we went away.

The people who were coming into the Wigtown house wanted to move in quickly, and Her tenant wasn't ready to move out of London, so She hired a nasty pink bungalow at the bottom of our old road and we lived there for a few weeks. It had been made entirely dogproof as the people who owned it had had a small apricot poodle, and wouldn't let him out on the road, so he turned into a sex maniac. The whole place was covered with tarmac which is very tiring to the feet, and a gate shut firmly with netting behind it. I could have gone mad there quite safely if I'd felt like it, but it was winter again and too cold. I generally stayed in with Her in the hideous kitchen, which had different patterns on the wallpaper and curtains and linoleum and none of them matched any of the others. She hated it as much as I did and I kept wondering why She didn't go back up the road to where our old cottage was, but She wouldn't. I expect it was partly because new people were in and partly because of the lost elm tree. It had been putting up shoots very bravely before we left but didn't look like it had once done, and She didn't want to go back. So we used to go up only far enough to see the farmer's wife who had brought the news about the Major, and have coffee. The only thing was that they had a brown collie named Tib, who was a bit too affectionate in general. When I wasn't there Tib would come roaring down, and jump at Her and once tore Her coat, purely out of affection. After that She always took me and that worked, because Tib turned tail and ran away. There was a little Cairn terrier named Trixie inside the house and she was a good watchdog like me, and had just had two tiny puppies the size of cockroaches. Trixie didn't mind me as she was too busy licking them clean.

As for other enemies, although they weren't really, it would only be carpet salesmen or people looking for antique furniture and china dogs. She had a pair but wasn't parting with them. They are quite small with neat patches of white pottery shaved hair, and they sit together on the mantelpiece when there is one, alongside a ship in a bottle and a china shepherd and shepherdess in coloured clothes. We took them with us to London.

As for me, I had a drama of my own. Once we were in Dumfries on a very hot day and She had to park the car in the station square, as everywhere else was full because it was Wednesday and that is the day when country people come in to do their shopping. She asked if I would like to come and buy some large flowerpots, and I replied by curling up on the car front seat, free of my belt. I didn't want to walk about in the heat, and I wished we were under a tree. She opened the right hand window as far as she could without letting me get out or be taken out by someone – not that that is likely to happen – and would have opened the left one as well, but there were two Alsatians there parked in an open Land Rover and showing the whites of their eyes, so She left that window shut. After She had gone it got hotter and hotter and in the end I lay down on the floor with my tongue out, panting, which is the way dogs sweat. By and large I prefer heat to cold, but this was extreme, and I heard the Land Rover drive away and envied the Alsatians for getting a breath of air. Presently a woman with a large bosom came and saw me lying panting on the floor. 'Look at this, Daphne,' she called to another woman and some children who were with her. 'A sweet little bull terrier dying of heat, and only one window open.'

They crowded their various bosoms at the window and kept away what air there was, and She came back and wondered what was going on and came to the car and looked in and said: 'Hello, Alice, I thought you were dead,' and started to get her car keys. The woman yelled 'It's a wonder she isn't dead, in this heat.'

Now I regret to state that She has a quick temper as far as humans are concerned. It is also possible that She was feeling the heat too, carrying flowerpots. I heard Her reply very rudely to the good lady, who began to threaten the police and the R.S.P.C.A. I wished I could speak up and tell them there was no need to make a fuss because there had been the Alsatians at the other window with whom I would almost certainly have come to grips. However She yelled back: 'Try it; you'll find they know me quite well,' because She always gives to the R.S.P.C.A. and goes to their coffee mornings. The woman shouted back 'I dare say they do,' which was a good exit line. We got out of the hot station square and as soon as the bosomy woman was out of sight She opened the other window, but hadn't done it while the woman was still there, on principle. When we got home I had a long drink of water and said 'Aarrgh' through my nose, which expressed a lot, and did an upward dive towards Her nose, but She knew enough by then to get away in time.

There were friends we used to go and see in Sussex called Spud and Ruth. They had a big garden which was fenced in all round because they had once bred

111

Afghans, who can never be taken out except on a lead because they are hunters. I myself think there are limits to a lead and merely sit down when I am tired of one. Anyhow, the last Afghan had been called Issa and if he liked people used to come and visit them in the middle of the night – he used to visit Her there before I came – so all the doors were left open. By now Issa was dead and Spud and Ruth had been so sad without a dog that they had gone to the dogs' home and had found Donny, who is a cross between a Gordon setter and something else. Donny had a terrible history. He was still very thin in spite of Ruth's feeding, because he had been starved and ill-treated all his life and so had his mother. Because she hadn't been properly fed while he was still inside her with his brothers and sisters, he didn't have teeth that were any good at all for chewing; all his food had to be soft and he could never, for instance, enjoy a bone. He was still afraid of a great many things despite the fact that Spud and Ruth were kind to him, so of course he was afraid of me. He was afraid even of Spud's stick when Spud raised it to help himself out of his armchair. The mere sight of a raised stick made Donny run away and hide in a corner, something the same as I still do with the Spoon only much, much worse becauuse he was absolutely terrified and I am only pretending. He wouldn't as much as wag his tail when I was about, although I wagged mine at him furiously, but I must say all this

Caesar's Wife, by C. Ambler, from a very old print kindly lent by
Mr and Mrs John Carr

What we can do when inclined, Police trials, 1956.
*By kind permission of The Sport and General Agency, London,
and The Kennel Club*

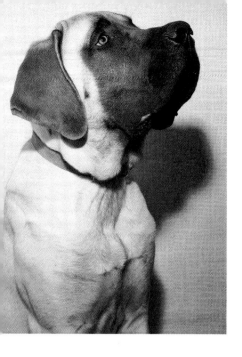

Janus as a puppy, and Magpie's (adult) daughter. Compare sizes!

Toughy

Ken's White Dog, ch. Megaror Moderator, *photograph Michael Trafford*

The only close-up of Alice, still very young, ears flattened because of the photographer *Maurice Bannister, Kirkcudbright*

Alice with Her

The cottage with Alice's apple tree, left

The pilgrimage road after
first tarring

Fred's relation. *By kind
permission of The Natural
History Museum, South
Kensington*

Early type bull terrier,
1804.
*Townley Stubbs,
owner unknown*

Wigtown Show, with the
Major and the Alsatian.
*By kind permission of
The Galloway Gazette,
Limited*

was partly my fault because I made it clear from the beginning who was going to be first with the food. Donny usually got ox cheek which is a very pleasant dish, and I even got into the habit of following Ruth about instead of Her, because while we stayed there that was where the grub came from. It was only a temporary arrangement. In the end Ruth used to feed me and Donny in separate rooms, otherwise he would have starved again. Also she took him out for walks in the early mornings by himself. I think long walks are overrated and nowadays when She tries to take me for one I simply go along till She lets me off the lead and then go back home and wait for Her. As regards the usual reason for being let out, there was once a neurotic visitor staying and whenever she saw me go outside she used to scream 'Pennies! Pennies! and I looked down my nose and pretended not to know what she was talking about. In my circles we call it going out to oblige, as I have tried to make clear: I like to call a spade a spade, but also I have a system I have perfected, of only providing halfpennies and having to be let out a second time, because that means I get two lots of chocolate drops instead of one.

Anyway it was pleasant staying with Spud and Ruth in Sussex and Spud used to scratch my back with his stick that had so frightened Donny. I missed the ox cheek when we got home again. In Scotland they use that and most of the liver and tripe and other interesting things to make into haggis and probably black pudding. I may sound a bit commercial about food in Sussex but it was a question of making hay while the sun shone. However we soon moved back to London.

I remember the last drive of all down from Scotland particularly because She had a very small car again, a Citroën CV6, bright blue, and in spite of all the worldly goods Dill and Hughie had taken in their van there seemed to be a lot left over. We really were like a salesman's van ourselves, not to mention a tinker's cart, stuffed with clothes and shoes and hats, rattling down the motorway. I had to fit in somewhere and did the sensible thing and slept most of the way on Her best hat. We stopped at service stations sometimes to eat and fill the car up with petrol – it was very economical and didn't use much – and one place was beside a lake and I went for a short walk with Her and we admired the scenery and I obliged. I don't mind walking if it is a new place and near at hand and I am let off the lead. Then we drove on and it was night before we got to London and everything was lit up and the yellow lights and traffic were very tiring, and She got lost so in the end She followed a 'bus that was going to Victoria. Every time the 'bus stopped we had to stop too. I think the conductor thought we were mad, but at one point he kindly waved us in the direction we were supposed to go. In the end we got to the flat at about three in the morning. An interesting thing had happened there. The tenant had for a long time refused to leave and it is sometimes difficult to get them out if they feel that way inclined, so in the end She had written to say *I am moving in with my bull terrier on Tuesday first* and the man said nothing more and fled.

We went down the funny old flight of steps and carried the bundles down and next day Dill and Hughie arrived with all the rest of the things from the pink bungalow that were ours, and a picture that wasn't. By degrees She got the place so that we could turn round, and in a day or two She went to the local electrician to ask if he knew of a good workman who would come and put the plugs right because they mostly didn't work. He told us about Mr Humphrey, which was a good thing, because many workmen in London won't come during the day and say they will come instead in the evenings and charge double, and it is called moonlighting. It was lucky we found out about Mr Humphrey because he is not only an electrician but a plumber and builder as well and his brother-in-law, who is called Bill, is a painter. They came during the day for as long as She wanted them and by the end the flat looked much nicer and everything worked. The only thing was that like certain others I have mentioned, Mr Humphrey was terrified of me and wouldn't come into any room where I was without asking, very politely, if I could be put somwhere else. So I sat for hours and hours on Her bed beside Balthasar the squint-eyed lion with the door shut and every so often She would appear and take me out on the lead (which I hate) and feed me and so on, and Mr. Humphrey pretended to shiver as I went past and said 'Yes, darling, yes, sweetheart, chomp, chomp, chomp,' as if he was a bone between my jaws. Bill however didn't mind me at all.

After the work was finished She put Her typewriter at Her old battered desk in the only sunny place in the flat, with the large corduroy armchair they'd only got in by removing its castors first and then putting them on again, for me beside Her. I sit by Her when She works if I feel like it, and if I do not I go away. It isn't like the cottage with its fields, and the garden, but on the other hand nobody runs me over because there is a No Entry sign at our end of the street.

That is one of the benefits, but on the other hand there isn't much daylight because it is a basement. I can sit in the dark sitting-room and look out for cats through the french windows to the patio, which by now are double-glazed as this is one of the improvements She had put in. I remember not to crash through them if and when I see a cat, but this does not often happen as by now, they know I am there. In any case She got Mr. Humprhey to put wire mesh round the garden lattice and fasten it at all the places where cats used to get through. Now the birds can come instead, but I don't chase birds. They eat the snails and so do I, so there is a certain rivalry, especially as the birds get there first in the early morning. However I have other things to eat.

That is at the back, and quite private. Outside at the front, once one has climbed the steps, there is a view of a block of flats for geriatrics, which is the dressed-up word for old people. Most of these knew me from the times before and call out 'Hello, Alice,' from their balconies on a fine day, like the people in Wigtown did once they got used to me. These London flats were built on bomb craters left over from the wartime blitz, and before that there used to be houses with pillars at the upper door, like ours except that we don't live in the rest of it, somebody else does. One block of the flats is called a hyrize and there are twenty floors. I certainly wouldn't like to have to live at the top.

The old people in fact miss very little that goes on, and at the beginning used to keep an eye on Her in case she wasn't a respectable person. However they decided She was all right, only they went on watching most things that happen here because it passes the time. This turned out to be a very good thing for me, as I shall relate.

The gallant little bright blue CV6 which had rattled us down to London with our belongings wasn't as useful in London as it had been in the country, because cars aren't. Rather than try and sell it – She is always swindled when She tries to sell anything, and Vi even beat down the agreed price of my puppies and got away with it – She decided to give it away to something which had helped Her very much inside Her mind. At first they wouldn't believe anyone really was giving them a car for nothing, and She had to keep on telephoning until She got hold of, as She put it, the horse's mouth. He asked like everyone else why She didn't sell it. 'In the first place I'm bad at selling things, and in the second place I loved it,' She said. 'If it sits out in the street somebody'll steal it or take the engine out.' So they took it away and kept it meantime in their car park and in the end after advertising in twenty magazines sold it to a collector, and bought themselves an internal telephone system with the change. I had an affection for that car as well, although it had been too cold to sit in and guard for long as it was strictly basic, with no luxuries for the passenger. Once the door blew off in Wigtown in a high wind, but luckily hit nobody. For some time it made a gap in our lives not to have it, but it is only possible to park without fuss on Sundays and so we got used to walking.

Preently the horse's mouth came round to thank Her and sat in my armchair. When he got up again after sitting chatting, his black coat – he was a priest – was covered with white hairs, and they were mine. It isn't that She doesn't brush me, but there they were.

118

'I'll get a clothes brush,' She said hastily, and went and got one and brushed and brushed, but the hairs didn't come off entirely. 'Alice's hairs are magnetic,' She said. The horse's mouth endured it all with great patience and said he'd pick the rest off by hand and keep them as souvenirs. It was his best coat and after that he used to come round in an old jersey, which wasn't as important.

I do not really like London. One thing I can never understand is that gutters have to be used instead of pavements. I also get extremely tired of walking on the lead and when I have had enough of it, sit down firmly, like Janus at Olympia. She gets cross then and lets me off it, which means I can oblige wherever I feel inclined. This is not popular. At one point She was advised to buy a thing called a Pooper Scooper which was said to be dispensed by the local council. She had to go to their offices and was asked what She wanted, said, 'I want a Pooper Scooper' and they looked at Her as though She was mad, because the news had not yet been delivered to all council departments. In the end She came home and said 'I had to go up six floors because of you and your Pooper Scooper, and when I paid for it it turned out to be made of cardboard and would have been perfectly disgusting to carry about after two goes. I gave it back to them and said we'd use newspaper.' We have done this to date and it works just as well and costs much less. She is economical in such ways, then suddenly buys Herself a hat with feathers. However, unless it is very early morning or late at night, London as I say is not the ideal place for a dog. A lot of people take theirs to Battersea Park, but She says there are macho dogs there that get into fights, and won't take me. As for the shops, they mostly have a notice saying NO DOGS so if She goes shopping, She leaves me at home and takes me out separately later on. One street is much like another, although the smells are different. This brings me to the story of the worst thing that ever happened to me, worse than the operations.

If She was in a hurry She would let me off the lead, for reasons already stated, and leave me to follow Her back home as I had done in Wigtown and was beginning to do here. One day for some reason we went further than usual, past the crossing of the second street. I wouldn't go past the third street, and She left me there to go to the shops. As I always do, I nosed along the railings, and there were interesting smells left by other dogs and some cats, and chocolate wrappers which I always like to investigate. One way and another when I got back to what should have been our gate, it wasn't. I began to try to find it and the harder I tried the worse it got, and there were a great many smells but none from Her footsteps, and I crossed crossings and poked in at gates and turned round and tried again and got mixed up and then started to look for the geriatric flats where everyone knew me. By this time quite a long time had passed and I thought She would have got back home and would start looking for me, which in fact by that time She was doing, but we didn't meet up.

In the end I found a block of flats which were the same as our geriatric ones to look at, but I didn't know them and they didn't know me. I stood in the entrance and didn't go in although there was some grass. She never lets me on to the geriatric estate grass as once one of the inmates, not a geriatric but a woman, called out rudely that this was a private estate in case we didn't know, and no dogs 'ere.

I waited for a long time. If I had only known, it wasn't so very far from our flat, but it was a side road I hadn't been taken to before and didn't remember any of the smells. I didn't know where to go next or what to do, and decided that the sensible thing to do was to stay where I was. As the Major used to say, bull terriers have bad noses. After all nobody can have everything.

It seemed a long time and I wished She would appear. Heads began poking out of windows and voices began to call, but none of them said Alice and I knew I was in the wrong place altogether. I heard someone say then 'Tell the porter. It must have strayed.' I am not used to being spoken of as it. Presently two young men came and looked to see if I had a name and address disc on my collar. Now, I have to admit that the one I had had in Scotland got worn and fell off, and neither She nor I had worried about replacing it, which is Her fault, but we were generally together and I suppose it hadn't occurred to Her that I would ever get lost. When the two men found I hadn't a name disc they said: 'Better take it to the station' which I afterwards found was Hyde Park Police Station. They got me into a car and drove with me through all kinds of unknown streets and at one point I saw a park, but wasn't let out there and one young man kept tight hold of my collar while the other drove.

We got to the station and a constable filled in forms about where I had been found and at what time and so on, and (this turned out to be important) that I was a bull terrier bitch, white, with a feather mark over one eye. Then I was taken away and put in a cell. I know some people laugh about having been in the cells but believe me, it wasn't funny. I couldn't get out and didn't know where I was, and there wasn't even a rug to lie on. I think they meant to treat me kindly and they brought me some water, but I wouldn't drink.

Soon it got dark and I knew She must be frantic with worry by this time, and some hours later – it seemed like days – a policeman came and took off my collar and put on another one, and put me in a van which was full of dogs. I cannot describe how dreadful it was to be in that van. It started up its engine and none of us knew where we were going or whom we were with. I didn't look at the dogs much but they were all different kinds, some of them abandoned like the rescued bull terriers at Ken and Mary's: you could tell from their eyes. I wondered if She had got in touch with the police because if She had, surely it would be all right in the end. But nothing happened and we drove and drove, and every time we stopped it was to take on more dogs. I found afterwards that they do this every so often, because there are hundreds of dogs abandoned every day in London. They are collected at the stations and then sent – as I found now – to Battersea Dogs' Home.

It was pouring with rain when I got there with the rest of them. We were let out all together by opening the back doors of the police van, and we didn't run but straggled out as if we were under an anaesthetic like I'd been that time at the vet's. Two young women in gumboots and overalls handled us and for once I didn't stand foursquare up to them. In fact I was very frightened. The place had a smell of fear, and I knew I was miles from home and so was everybody else, and what was going to happen to us I didn't know, and couldn't guess. I simply put on my deadpan expression and let them do as they liked with me. They put me in a cage. They put all of us into separate cages. There were passages between the cages and I could hear that there were dozens more, even cages in other houses next door across the yard where we had been let out.

But I didn't have to wait long. Almost the minute I was put in the cage She appeared and saw me, and said: 'That's Alice. I never thought I would see her again.' I trotted out and She took me outside to where She had a taxi waiting and everybody at the Home, all the humans I mean, stood and smiled and watched us go off. They are always very pleased when a dog is reclaimed, because otherwise they have to find it a new home within a certain time or else put it kindly down.

Afterwards She told me what had happened to Her. She was still all wet, even Her hair, becuse she had walked twice to Battersea that morning and had been taken round all the cages already and hadn't found me because I was still in the van. 'There was another bull terrier there,' She said, 'but he wasn't you. I walked back through Battersea Park and felt as though life had come to an end. There are places for dogs to run there. I wish we'd kept the car and then you could perhaps come, but you wouldn't walk as far now, and there are the machos.' But I didn't care about Battersea Park or machos or about anything except that I was back with Her again.

It is really amazing how there is a grapevine in town as well as in the country. When She couldn't find me She told the police, but a different station, and asked everybody including the people on the geriatric balcony if they'd seen me. There was a man there called Robert who is on crutches, and he'd heard from the porter that they'd taken me to the police station and then to Battersea Home. Unfortunately She had gone straight away to the Home before I got there, and had to come back, and had gone round all the shops and places again afterwards, and had offered a reward, but no good. Then Robert came over on his crutches and the Home telephoned Her to say a dog answering to my description had just been brought in. So She got a taxi just as She was, like a drowned rat, and came straight away, and now She is a Friend of Battersea Dogs' Home because if it wasn't there, even worse things would happen to stray dogs, including perhaps being used for laboratory experiments. 'I was terrified that might be done,' She said. 'I didn't know about Battersea Home until Robert told me that's where you probably were.'

So there it is, but as had happened after the operation long ago, I was different, this time in my mind. It was a long time before I would go out on the street again, and only agreed to go and oblige in the back garden. She understood and didn't try to force me to go out. Then She began lettng me run up the steps to the shut gate, and then one day, still with me, She left the gate open. I went out on the pavement a little way and then came back. After that, very, very slowly, I got back my confidence and by now would walk on the streets again alone, only She won't let me. She gets the shopping separately and then takes me out for a special walk, twice daily, with a lead in Her hand just in case.

However, shortly the same kind of thing happened to Her as well, only worse. Before that, there was The Last Cruise.

Six

Once when She was on one of these I disapproved of and I was staying with Sheila and Mark and the ghost, She saw a thing which made Her decide never to go abroad again. It happened on Sardinia, where they had stopped to visit things and places. One was a church in the middle of nowhere called the Church of the Holy Cow, because long ago a cow was supposed to have appeared in the evenings to feed the starving missionaries on milk. Not far off was a strange stone building, very ancient, called a nuarghe. It was shaped like a flask with a narrow top and had small narrow openings for light near the ground and in the upper part. Long ago early peoples used to protect themselves inside it in time of war or attack. Most of the party went up the inside steps to the upper floors to see the view from the bottle top, but She, of course, had to be different and went to explore the dark ground-floor passages.

She hadn't gone far when She came across a dog. It was lying with its head on its paws, in the dark, waiting to die. It must have dragged itself for miles across the dry scrub where there was no shade or water at all, to find the only place to be alone and cool. It was black-and-white, and had some bull terrier blood. It must have come from the Costa Smeralda, the rich man's playground miles off on the coast; there wasn't anywhere nearer. She knelt down by it and, very gently, stroked it to show someone was there who loved dogs, as in those places they don't. Afterwards She remembered staring at an old wound low on its side, dried and turned back in a black scar long ago. It had been knifed, and had somehow managed to live for a long time since.

She didn't want to lift it on to the sill of the slit through which it must have come, but soon the rest would come down and would disturb it. However it seemed there was no need; as She stroked it it slowly stretched out its long whippy tail quite straight, as dogs do when they die. She stood up and found one of the party there already.

'You shouldn't have touched it,' he said. 'It may have rabies.' However She didn't care, and anyway it hadn't been a rabid dog; all it had wanted was to die quietly in the dark. She went away, as there seemed nothing to be done. After leaving the nuarghe they stopped somewhere else a few miles further on, and She heard two young men on the coach laughing and saying 'The best thing of the lot was that dead dog that wasn't dead.'

She turned round; they were the sort who don't care about much except themselves. 'You're sure it was alive?' She asked, and they went on laughing and said it had been quite definitely alive. She realised then that the movement of its tail hadn't meant death; it had been trying to wag it. Since then it had been disturbed, sick and in torment, forced to move again, the place of quiet darkness invaded and spoilt. It would happen again and again, as there would be coach parties to the nuarghe all day.

She went at once to the driver, who spoke a little English, and asked him if there was anywhere on the island that cared for animals, such as the RSPCA. He stared at Her as though She was mad. 'They are there, but will not come out,' he said. 'Men are killed on the roads, and nobody does anything.'

She didn't care about that, and went to the tour

organiser, who very kindly got a special car and drove back with a friend to find out what had happened to the dog. They returned to say that a nun in the next party was sitting with it and had said '*Moribunda.*'

She had known it was dying, but not that it was a bitch; She hadn't taken time to look one way or the other in the dark. To have knifed a bitch was unspeakable. 'What could I have done?' She asked me afterwards. 'The nun would have to go when her own party left, and what happened to it then? If I'd known I would have stayed with it, but they wouldn't have let me take it back on board ship, because of their regulations.' She thought about that dog all up the coast of Portugal and long afterwards. She went to the ship's doctor and said 'Charge me a consultation fee, but how long will it take to die?' He said comfortingly that it would certainly be dead by now, and wouldn't take any money, but She still wasn't certain and as soon as She got home, even before sending for me, wrote to the papers telling them what had happened and begging breeders not to sell dogs to Latin countries. *The Telegraph* published Her letter but *The Times* by then wouldn't, as they said it was no longer exclusive news.

Seven

I had noticed for a long time that She was a bit tense and getting peculiar, but we all have our oddities or the world wouldn't be such an interesting place. However when She began to hear music that hadn't been written yet and to see things that weren't there and burst out laughing about what She couldn't remember five minutes later, it began to get worrying. I believe they call it the stress syndrome, and it involved a great many things that had happened in the years before I knew Her, probably from the time She was born. She didn't of course sleep at all without pills, and these got stronger and stronger and after we came to London to a new doctor who didn't know Her, he said nobody ought to be taking all those and stopped the lot. As a result, She went crazy. She changed her doctor, but by then it was too late. One day She went out and didn't come back, and I waited and waited and it began to get dark. I drank all the water in my bowl but there wasn't any food, and I was getting hungry, but that didn't matter so much as wondering if She had lost Herself or else been taken away in a plain van.

After a long time there was the sound of the key in the lock. Our locks are very good against burglars but an inspector who came at the beginning looked at me and said to Her 'She's your best investment.' I felt very pleased at the time, but didn't seem to be much of an investment now. Two people walked in and they were the police. I did my duty and stood foursquare and looked them in the eye.

'Something'll have to be done about *that*,' said one officer to the other, who replied that the woman next door had said she'd take me. Evidently the geriatrics knew all about everything as usual and had reported Her as behaving very strangely in the street. She had been taken away not in a plain van, but a police one. There is a first time for everything. She was evidently now in a hospital for those afflicted with their nerves. I learned this from the woman next door, who was called Winifred and who fed me the best fish from the beginning of our acquaintance. It occurs to me now that but for Winifred and the police, I might have starved to death. As it was, once I knew what had happened to Her, I put up with the situation until She should be let out again.

Win lived in a house with purple pillars as she is an individualist and won't paint them cream colour like everyone else. It was the first time I had set eyes on her as London is not like the country and you don't know your neighbours, even the ones next door. In a way this is a good thing, but now She was as nutty as a fruit cake for the time being, I was glad to move in with Win. Win had four cats but they made themselves scarce, and as it was a large house there was plenty of room for all and sundry. I simply got on with life and waited for Her to come back from round the bend, and Win went to see Her in hospital and tell Her I was all right, then came back and told me She was, more or less.

'She's getting back to normal,' Win told me, adding that it would be a matter of weeks. I knew that what would bother Her more than anything was having to be in a ward with other people, as She likes to be by herself with, of course, my company. Even on cruises She insists on a single cabin, which costs extra. However there it was.

Time passed, and I used to go out into Win's back yard which is full of weeds and cat smells, and now and again a neighbour would call who has five rescue dogs on long leads, but he didn't bring them in. We used to meet all sorts of characters, She and I, on our walks. There was somebody who called himself the Bionic Man. He had had three pacemakers and two metal knees and shoulder joints and two new hips, and he used to get about on crutches with a rescued Pekingese on a long lead somehow as well. I cannot think who would ill-treat a Pekingese.

One day I knew She had come back next door, because I heard her voice faintly, but it wasn't for good and somebody had brought Her for what they call a rehabilitation visit. It wasn't a success as the person kept calling and calling Her name, as though She had been a stray dog, and I knew this would drive her even further round the bend than ever and almost barked to try to get the other person to stop, but didn't. It was a nasty feeling to know She was there and yet not quite all there, if you follow. They went away, and I heard Her say 'They've drunk the Chianti.'

I knew who They were, because I'd heard them too; they came back again, and this time they replaced the Chianti in case they were copped, but they stole books She didn't notice were missing till long afterwards, and left the immersion heater on for five weeks and didn't replace that, and filled the kitchenette sink with dirty cups and left the plug in and the tap dripping, so that when She was allowed back out at last the flat was an inch deep in water and the carpets were soaking. It wasn't that they were very valuable, it was the principle of the thing.

Worst of all, they had found Her jewel case and had been careful not to take any of the jewels as those could be traced, but they'd found the Major's letters and read them and then put them back in the wrong envelopes, which is how She knew. When She came back She sold the jewels, as once it is known you have things like that somebody's relations may break in, in spite of the presence of myself. Anyway She didn't often wear jewels any more by then.

Meantime, as they still hadn't let Her back out, I simply went on eating the best fish. I will say it gave me ideas I had not had previously. In fact, as She discovered slightly too late, there is VAT on pet food but not on human food, so it is cheaper to feed us on the best of everything. The butcher sells excellent smoked ham.

Anyway one day – it had seemed such a long time that I was almost used to it – I was with Win in her back yard hanging out washing, which we aren't supposed to do in our locality as it lowers the tone. Suddenly a head appeared over the wall and it was Hers. She must have been standing on the brick surround that keeps in the flower beds round our patio, not that any flowers grow because of cats in the small hours. 'Would you like Alice back?' Win asked politely, and She said yes, please, so I was brought round and She had the sense to pay Win at once for all the fish I'd consumed, which came to £60. After Win had gone I was about to do my round-and-round dance to show I was pleased, but She came and put her arms round me hard and said 'Alice, Alice,' which meant a great many things.

Since then we have continued as usual. She mostly takes me out at night as I think I have said, because of finding pavements more comfortable than gutters and then using newspaper. Several other dog owners have the same idea, except for one man who is always drunk and drags his dog along using a four-letter word and waking everyone up and using the pavements anyway. Otherwise there is an enormous and very beautiful Harlequin Great Dane and a greyhound and the Bionic Man and his Pekingese, who is called Chang. Chang told me his ancestors used to sit in the sleeves of emperors.

There was one dog I only saw once, and never again. He was not allowed to make friends with anyone. He had been bred to guard property, but he wasn't an Alsatian or anything in particular, but a mixture of everything, not by chance but on purpose. One of his forebears may have been the ghost dog Henry who had been run over and killed long ago and was by now really a ghost. This dog was the same grey colour, and a sad and terrible sight. He was part St. Bernard and so was very large, with red drooping eyelids, and pricked-up ears and a double chin, with some Dobermann as well. He was taken round very fast and then hustled away. I was sorry for him and so was She; the owner wouldn't even tell Her the dog's name. 'He can't have any life,' She said to me afterwards. 'Why didn't they get a bull terrier? That would have done the job just as well.'

By then, She was more or less all right again.

* * *

She wrote to the hospital complaining about the books that had been taken, but there was no reply. She wrote again twice and then got a solicitor. The hospital answered then and said the personnel concerned had gone long ago and She should have got in touch earlier. 'I suppose it might have been worse; they might have set the place on fire,' She said, and paid the solicitor's bill.

The next thing was, believe it or not, another piano. This was partly because the priest who'd got my hairs all over his best coat was appointed to a church where he needed an organist. She persuaded Herself that She could do the job if She practised on a piano in advance, and remembered one left to her by a great-aunt when She was fifteen and which in the days when She was poor, She had sold to an

education committee for £35, which in those days was a good deal of money. Somebody told Her that by now the piano in question would be matchwood, but She wrote off to the committee, which was in Scotland, and got a letter back to say that they preferred to leave matters as they were. She wrote again pointing out the circumstances and that her great-aunt had been a pupil of a pupil of Liszt and that for sentimental reasons She would like to have it back, and would replace it with one of equal value. Then they wrote back to say that one of equal value would cost £1,000. 'I suppose I'm a fool,' She said to me, 'but Liszt met Beethoven and Beethoven met Mozart and Mozart only just missed Bach, so it's a link.' I said nothing, because there was nothing to say.

The piano was bought back, to the tune they'd asked, but the next job was to get it into the flat and, in fact, to London at all. If She had had any sense, which She hasn't, She would have got professional piano movers to collect it straight from the school where it was, but instead She had got Her friend Mr. Dill to take it away for old times' sake, and he kept ringing up to say it would have to be a part load and he wasn't coming down meantime, but was keeping it warm with an electric bulb. In fact, as She told me afterwards, this was not a good idea. Pianos can stand a good deal of damp and cold, and once in the early days at the cottage, before it had a damp course or I arrived, She had come back to find it bright blue with mould, but still playing. It was a Broadwood and had been made in 1914, when pianos were tough.

In the end She found professional piano movers after all, who swore they went round there every week by way of Ireland. They said they would collect the Broadwood from Wigtown with ease, but they tried and tried and Mr. Dill never seemed to be at home. She rang him up and he said both he and his wife had waited in, but they hadn't come for it, and business was business. Time passed in such ways, and in the end She told Mr. Dill for goodness' sake to bring it down as a single load, which he said would cost £350.

This was agreed, but just then scaffolding was put up at street level because builders were working on some brickwork to improve matters generally. When Mr. Dill and Hughie arrived with the piano by itself in a large van, they had to take it to pieces and lay every single note out separately on the pavement – luckily it wasn't raining – and try to get the other bits downstairs somehow. This wasn't easy because of the scaffolding, and the builders wouldn't undo this because of something called third party insurance.

In the end She had to pay the builders to help with the piano as well, as it was heavy and the front door is narrow with an angle at the turn, and Mr. Dill kept saying there was a 90% chance of getting it in at all, which She knew already as they had discussed measurements frequently over the telephone. It came down the steps at last with dreadful creaks and groans as it was squeezed past the wall, and She was saying Her prayers and I was keeping right out of the way, as was tactful. In the end it just got past, that is to say the main part, and presently Mr. Dill and Hughie brought down the notes from the pavement and put them in place again wth a good deal of heavy breathing and calculation. After they had gone She found that most of them were back in the wrong places in spite of being numbered on the back with a B pencil. Also, there was a large piece missing which represented the entire lower part of the piano's stomach. She rang up Mr. Dill, who by that time was back in Scotland, and he swore the missing part wasn't in his store and wasn't in his van. It certainly wasn't on the pavement. In the end She got a carpenter who made a new panel with magnetic clips, as there was no other way of disguising the piano's large intestine. She also got a tuner who put the notes back in the right places and who turned out to be descended from the murderer of the Princes in the Tower. This is the kind of thing that happens to Her, especially in London.

By that time, the priest had got himself a guitar player anyway and didn't need an organist after all. She tried to play the piano for a bit and I tried not to make my A flat minor howl to show Her how extremely second-rate Her playing is. It is one of the things She shouldn't do. However although She made a great fuss for some time about taking illegal photocopies of Bach from the library and playing *Bist du bei mir* till I got sick of it, the piano turned out to be handy for keeping scripts on and then couldn't be opened without shifting them again. So She belted up at last and there was peace. That is a good thing as regards money as well, because at that rate She makes enough to pay for my smoked ham from the butcher. I like it even better than fish, which She is too lazy to cook or take out the bones.

Dogs like to doze off at about three in the afternoon if they are left in peace, and She took up the habit Herself sooner or later. Humans in general got the idea from us and call it The Siesta. She used to throw a cover over herself and lie down for a couple of hours to think out the next chapter, having put Balthasar on the floor. I would go along to the bedroom, push open the door with my nose, then bulldoze upwards under the cover to the level of Her knee, then settle there. 'You're as good as a hot water bottle,' She used to say. She then finished Her siesta and I finished mine. It is not the same as sleeping. I suppose you could call it a recharging of batteries, like the Major used to have done for his electric chair by means of a thing he kept on the cellar wall at his farm. She tried to switch it on for him once and switched the wrong thing and everything exploded.

It seemed a long time since the Major had died. Sometimes I would think about dying myself. It happens to everybody, after all, and there is no point in getting worked up. I used to wonder, and still do, if I would meet the mastiff Janus and the little black-and-white chihuahua Magpie, and Biddy, and the others She had had before I came, and if we would all wait together like a reception comittee for when She came along in due course. On the other hand perhaps bull terriers keep themselves to themselves up there the way they do down here, and in that case perhaps I would meet up with the Major's dog Tony, the one he had had to put down because of the war. Perhaps the Major would be there too. It was something to look forward to, after all. I know She believes we all go on, although the Major didn't.

We do not in fact live as long as most dogs. I know She hadn't thought about this and would be sad again when I'd gone. However there is nothing to be done in that way, as although some breeds live till sixteen or more in human terms, bull terriers have been bred to live so intensely they can't expect quantity as well as quality. I do not expect to be different, and I would have liked to get Her used to the idea that She would not have me with Her for ever. I tried one day to fix Her with my eyes from my basket, which She bought me so that She can sometimes sit in the armchair Herself. I think She knew I was trying to say something special, because She looked back and didn't say anything, which is the right answer.

I don't suppose that at Her time of life She will get another bull terrier, and certainly not a puppy. At that rate She might die before it did, which is a thing dog owners ought to consider and often don't. Others buy a puppy for the children at Christmas and then when it has stopped being cuddly, drive it out somewhere and abandon it because they are tired of it. I will say that whatever else, She has never got tired of me. I saw to the matter personally.

Eight

Ever since I had been lost and taken to the Dogs'
Home in Battersea She had taken an interest in it, and
quite right too. Every year they have an Annual
General Meeting either there, or at their annexe at
Bell Mead near Windsor. It is of course nothing to do
with it that they give Her and the others a really
excellent tea, with different varieties of cakes and
scones and biscuits. All kinds of people go including
a belted earl and a former airline pilot, who was badly
injured in a crash but still gets himself there every
year. There is also a dog who attends with his owner
and who barks at the right moment to show his
agreement in course of proceedings.

She didn't take me to Bell Mead, as She thought,
rightly, that I wouldn't want to see or smell more
dogs in cages. However She told me all about it when

She got back and said 'I saved you a scone,' which was pleasant. She also told me about the dogs She had seen there and was of course tempted as usual to buy, but remembered my feelings. 'There was the sweetest little Staffordshire who'd been ill-treated, and she was still trusting and friendly,' She said. The man who showed them around said not to worry, she'd be found a good home, but it doesn't follow that dogs forget what has happened to them.

Otherwise, there was a specal puppy house, as Bell Mead takes whelping bitches and finds homes for the litters after they have been weaned. When the puppies are old enough they have great fun in a long blue tunnel they can chase through and come out at the other end, round and round, and there are toys for them to play with. Bell Mead is a beautiful place full of old trees and a house where the offices are, and grass runs below for the dogs when they are brought out by people who want to have a look with a view to buying them. As I have said already, they won't be allowed to do so if they aren't suitable, and afterwards things are kept an eye on until it is certain the dog is happy and well looked after. This is very important work, and so is the campaign to stop people buying a puppy for Christmas and then leaving it somewhere on a strange road when they are tired of it. A puppy is not a present for children, unless the children are certain not to be cruel. Often they do not mean this, but at other times they do.

146

Some people think animals are unimportant and that more money should be spent on humans and less on dogs and cats and horses and donkeys and dolphins and whales. To this She always says – it is one of Her few sensible sayings – that cruelty and indifference to created things lowers humanity and insults God. One person who understood this was St. Francis of Assisi, who got a fierce wolf to follow him into a village because all it wanted was food. He made the villagers promise to leave food out for it after he had gone, and there was no more trouble. Most animals are like this. They will kill for food, but not because they like killing for its own sake. A cat plays with a mouse to start up its own digestive juices, not to be particularly unkind. However the mouse no doubt has separate views on the matter.

I have been well fed all my life, and nobody has been cruel to me on purpose, not even the people who ran me over. I suppose I am having a benevolent old age.

There are a great many places in London which won't let dogs in, and even when She had Her chihuahua it was counted as a dog even though it was held up against Her and didn't touch the floor. This is fair in places like food shops, I suppose, knowing the habits of some. However one day it was snowing, and She said 'Alice, I want some whisky,' which doesn't really go with Her sleeping pills but never mind. For once

147

we went to the local pub. There are a great many in this part of the world, some with old names and some with new ones. The first pub wouldn't let Her in with me, so we swept off and went to another. That one used to be called The Monster because there was once a monastery there instead, but not everybody knows this and as had happened with the Ancient British boar Fred at midnight on the bridge long ago, people expected to see something like a dinosaur if they had had a drop too much, so by now it was called something else. They didn't say we couldn't come in, so we went, and a man sitting beside another one drinking beer as we passed by said 'Beautiful dog. Bull terrier.' That was a much better attitude, and if we made a habit of frequenting pubs we would go to that one again and not the other.

She had Her whisky and we went home in the snow. Another day, after it had melted, we were

walking down the next street and an old gentleman was standing at his front door and looked at me and said 'Oh, you beauty.' That cheered me up no end, because as already related I have a metal leg and a metal shoulder and an operation scar, not to mention the bald place where the Major's Alsatian bit me long ago. However my ears are like the sails of a yacht, and my nose black by now like my mother's, and I have what is called a good head and know how to carry myself. If things had turned out differently I could have spent a miserable life being shown. I might even have won a few rosettes, but this is of no importance.

I am getting on for seventy now in dog terms, and I don't go as far or charge about as much as I used to and am quite glad to settle down in the velvet armchair or else against the stuffed lopsided lion Balthasar on the bed. It makes me quite happy if one day goes by exactly like the next. Friday is a special day because She goes to the market and brings me back a pound of chicken necks and a pound of chicken hearts, from the stall at the market. I get wholemeal biscuits, of course; otherwise I get different kinds of tinned meat as well as the ham, sometimes flavoured with liver or kidney or tuna, or beef and heart. I regret to say it is cats' meat really as I prefer it to the kind they make for dogs. Sometimes She goes to get it from a pet shop despite VAT and comes back and tells me about the Persian kittens and macaws and a cockatoo they have for sale, only She didn't buy any because of me, at least that is what She says. She gets me some green herbal pills there also as at times I rush about looking for something green to eat, but won't touch vegetables if She tries to give them to me. The pills don't matter one way or another but I take them to please Her because She is getting on as well.

One day we really excelled ourselves and got as far as Buckingham Palace for the Changing of the Guard. The railings were packed with people, tourists and many of them Americans, and we heard the band playing as the Guards came down the Mall and saw the scarlet uniforms and great black busbies they wear on their heads. She tells me these are not made of bearskin like they used to be, because it so heavy and nylon is lighter. I don't know how She finds out about things like that. Anyway there were commands shouted and marching and snapping to attention and saluting and forming fours, and I tried to watch between the people's legs but couldn't see much, and besides a great many of them were looking not at the guard but at Me. There was the usual question: 'Is it a bulldog?' and I stood foursquare on my two metal legs and two real ones and looked them in the eye and She told them I was a bull terrier. Then they asked my name, and She said I was Alice the Palace from Buckingham Palace and everybody laughed and some children came over and patted me. And that is all I have to say for the present.

Postscript by The Woman

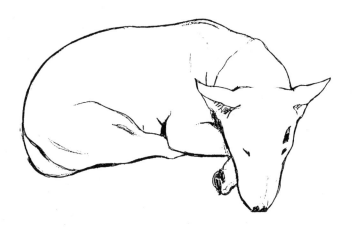

Alice died in her favourite velvet armchair just before
Christmas, 1989. She was twelve years old, which is as long
as bull terriers can expect to live. Sadly I was not with her,
but in any case she died in her sleep. As a friend said, there
was nothing that could have been done; but I should have
liked to be there.

Some time before, she had given me a certain clear wise
look from her basket. Dogs know when they will die soon; I
have met it in others. I could see the red glow of the retina
behind Alice's eyes in a way that was not visible as a rule; it
was almost as if her inmost soul – dogs have souls – was
putting out a message to me saying 'Well, here it comes;
we've done our best together, and I'll expect you when you
come after me.'

I had gone out only briefly, as I thought, but had been
delayed: they wanted to make a second recording of carols
for the BBC. I hurried home, and called out our usual
nonsense word, and Alice would always give her little bark

of welcome and stay, these days, where she was. This time there was no answer. When I reached the sitting-room, I noticed first that her nose, for the only time, was snub. It was snuggled deep in the chair's velvet arm, and she was dead. At first I could not believe it; she had been so much a part of my life, so much of life itself, having shared so many things and understood them all. I could hardly remember a time without her, her common sense and courage, loyalty and humour and tremendous fun. She had been wiser than humans are. Early that morning I had, somewhat half-heartedly, taken her out for her walk; she loathed leads and in the end, as there was nobody about, I let her off it. She gave her little skip of joy, the last; nosed about for a bit, then was ready to come home out of the cold. I knew she would settle in the armchair as soon as I left, because either I sat in it or else she did. It still has the mark where her nose sank down into the velvet after she was dead, becoming no longer Roman.

Neigbours called to condole, as though it had been a human death. The man with five strays came and tried to get me to take another dog immediately. I declined; no other dog would be Alice. Since then I have thought once or twice about taking another, which would have to be a bull terrier – nobody who has known one wants anything else – and I have looked at one or two and at times been tempted, epecially when one of them did a round-and-round dance of pleasure at being taken notice of. In a way this made it worse instead of better; to try to replace Alice was after all impossible. There simply never will be another of her, and so

I decided that I would write down her story from the beginning, though of necessity some of mine is tied up with it. I hope that you have liked reading about her.

I hope also that, if you decide you can understand and cope with a bull terrier, you will buy a puppy or else a rescued one. The latter will probably be a dog; bitches are seldom abandoned. The dogs are very strong, and if you let him get out of hand at the beginning, there will be endless trouble. On the other hand if you train him properly, and put up with a good deal in the process, he will delight you. If you are not prepared to put up with his exhibitions of character, leave him where he is. He will be well looked after meantime, and will not be given to anyone but the right person. The Dogs' Home, Battersea, or their annexe out at Bell Mead, Windsor (the one where Alice got her scone for tea) or any bull terrier rescue centre, whose addresses can be got from the Kennel Club, are all available; but they will look you over and ask you a great many questions, and may refuse to let you have the dog. Remember that, if he has been rescued, he has been betrayed once. If you take him, do not betray him again.

For me, there will as I say never be another Alice. Perhaps anyone may say the same thing about a dog who was particularly special. However a special bull terrier is more special than anything, as Alice would certainly have agreed, diving upwards with her nose.

Other publications from The Vineyard Press

SAINTS' NAMES FOR CONFIRMATION